Learning Through Play

Also available from Continuum

Behavioural, Emotional and Social Difficulties: A Guide for the Early Years, Janet Kay

Childminder's Guide to Play and Activities, Allison Lee

Childminder's Handbook, Allison Lee

Co-ordinating Special Educational Needs: A Guide for the Early Years, Damien Fitzgerald

Good Practice in the Early Years, Janet Kay

The Inside Guide to Being a Childminder, Allison Lee

Medical Conditions: A Guide for the Early Years, Pam Dewis

Observing Children and Young People, Carole Sharman, Wendy Cross and Dianna Vennis

Protecting Children, Janet Kay

Teaching Assistant's Handbook: Primary Edition, Janet Kay

Teaching 3–8, Mark O'Hara

Learning Through Play

A Work-Based Approach for the Early Years

Jacqueline Duncan and
Madelaine Lockwood

continuum

Continuum International Publishing Group

The Tower Building   80 Maiden Lane, Suite 704

11 York Road   New York, NY 10038

London

SE1 7NX

www.continuumbooks.com

British Library Cataloguing-in-Publication Data

A catalogue record for this book is available from the British Library.

ISBN: 9781847061683 (paperback)

Library of Congress Cataloging-in-Publication Data

Duncan, Jacqueline.

  Learning through play : a work-based approach for the early years / Jacqueline
Duncan and Madelaine Lockwood.

    p. cm.

 Includes bibliographical references and index.

 ISBN-13: 978-1-84706-168-3 (pbk.)

 ISBN-10: 1-84706-168-0 (pbk.)

 1. Play. 2. Early childhood education—Curricula. 3. Preschool teachers—In-service
training. I. Lockwood, Madelaine. II. Title.

 LB1140.35.P55D86 2008

 155.4'18—dc22

          2007036524

Typeset by Free Range Book Design & Production Limited

Printed and bound in Great Britain by Cromwell Press Ltd, Wiltshire

This book is dedicated to
Amy, Holly, James and Michael, whose play has fascinated, educated and delighted us.

Acknowledgments

The authors would like to acknowledge:

Woodthorpe Childminding Network, York, for their helpful comments on the text.
Particular thanks go to the staff, parents and children at Carr Infant School, York,
High Bentham Community Primary School, Lancaster and West Garth Primary School,
Marske by the Sea, for their time and generous permission to use images of the children's play.
Also thanks to Hob Moor Community Primary School, York and
High Bentham Community Primary, Lancaster, for trialling materials.

The authors would also wish to thank York St John University and
in particular colleagues in the Faculty of Education and Theology for their support.

Finally thanks must go to our husbands for their constant support and encouragement.

Contents

Introduction   1
The book structure and content   2
How to use this book   3
Professional development activities   4
Starting the journey   11
Further Reading, References   13

Part One How Children Learn

1 The Role of the Adult: Making Observations and Understanding the Child   17
Introduction   17
The role of the practitioner as observer in understanding children's play   18
What is observation?   18
Why observe children play?   19
A framework for effective observation   21
Ethics   24
Summary, Jargon explained, Further reading, References   27

2 The Child as a Thinker and Learner   30
Introduction   30
The brain and learning   31
Children construct their own understanding   33
The role of representation, language and interaction in learning   36
Learning starts from where the child is   41
Scaffolding   42
The spiral curriculum   43
Multiple intelligences   44
Learning dispositions and child involvement   44
Active learning   46
Schema   46
Further study   49
Summary, Further reading, References   49

3   Aspects of Development: Influences on Learning   54
   Introduction   54
   The influence of social and cultural contexts in which the child is developing   55
   The influences on development: relationships, stimulation, health, gender, environment
      and play   56
   How development affects learning and dispositions to learning   61
   Play and its influence on children's learning   63
   Summary, Jargon explained, Further reading, References   67

4   Key Ideas that Inform us about Learning Through Play   70
   Introduction   70
   Young children are competent and experienced learners   72
   Children's learning is influenced by significant others   73
   Language is a central mechanism in learning   75
   Learning can be scaffolded   78
   Observation can help us understand and support children's thinking   79
   Learning and development in one area can affect learning in all others   79
   Children learn best when actively involved in learning   80
   Jargon explained, References   82

Part Two Play and its Role in Pre-school Education

5   Play and Learning   85
   Introduction   85
   What do we mean by play?   86
   Play in the educational context   87
   How does good quality play support learning?   91
   What do we mean by good quality play?   95
   Key aspects of play   96
   Types of play and their importance   98
   Summary, Further reading, References   103

6   Developing the Context: Making Sense of Your Setting   105
   Introduction   105
   Evaluation against key principles   106
   The role of the practitioners in play   110
   Personal development   111
   Further reading   112

Part Three Key Principles for Developing and Supporting Play

7 The Role of the Practitioner: Monitoring and Assessment of Children's
Learning Through Play   115
Introduction   115
Defining monitoring and assessment   116
Reasons for monitoring and assessing children's play   116
Key principles for monitoring and assessing children's learning through play 118
Approaches and procedures for monitoring and assessment   122
Exemplar for assessment and recording   126
Summary, Further reading, References   132

8 The Learning Environment: Provision and Resources   134
Introduction   134
Why is the physical learning environment important?   135
What makes a quality play environment?   137
Planning provision areas   146
Summary, Jargon explained, References   152

9 The Role of the Adult in Supporting Sustained Meaningful Play:
Intervention   154
Introduction   154
What do we mean by intervention?   156
Why intervene?   157
What intervention strategies do settings adopt?   157
How can we intervene successfully?   159
What approaches might we adopt?   161
When might we choose not to intervene?   174
Jargon explained, Further reading, References   176

10 Planning: Developing a Framework for Children's Learning Through Play 179
Introduction   179
Defining planning for play   180
Reasons for planning play   180
The planning for play continuum   181
Key principles for planning children's learning through play   181
The planning for play process   184
Summary, Jargon explained, Further reading, References   196

X Contents

Part Four Management, Evaluation and Development of Quality Pre-school Provision

11 The Role of the Adult: Leadership and Management 201
Introduction 201
The role of the practitioner in leading and managing learning through play 202
Key principles and frameworks for the effective management and leadership
   of learning through play 204
Summary, Jargon explained, Further reading, References 218

12 Developing Your Context: Where Do We Go from Here? 221
Introduction 221
The improvement cycle: a framework for improving play in your setting 222
Envisioning the play provision for your setting 224
Completing an audit 224
Writing a policy for play 226
Writing a development plan for play 226
Writing action plans for play 227
Evaluation 228
Personal learning and development 229
Summary, Further reading, References 231

Appendices

1. Policy for play: what do we want for our children? 232
2. Development plan for play 236
3. An example of an action plan for developing an aspect of your
   development plan for play 237
4. Additional frameworks for supporting the development of play 238
5. What the research says: key research projects in this area 241
6. Current government documentation 245

Index 247

Introduction

Chapter Outline

The book structure and content   2
How to use this book   3
Professional development activities   4
Starting the journey   11
Further reading, References   13

This book is firmly based on the authors' beliefs about children and the nature of learning in the early years. It takes as a given that it is the nature of children to want to learn and that they learn best when they are actively engaged and are supported by adults who are knowledgeable about them and about their learning. It is aimed at all early years practitioners, in whatever setting, who want the best for the children in their care and who understand how important their role is in the life of the individual child and through that child in the future of our society as a whole.

Some have argued that play is children's work but it is far more than this. Play is their self-actualization, a holistic exploration of who and what they are and know and of who and what they might become (Broadhead 2004: 89).

This book is about children learning through play and about the role of the adult in this process. It has three overall aims: to help practitioners to become more skilful and imaginative when they are engaged in providing playful learning; to support the development of excellent contexts for learning through play; and to help practitioners to become confident and articulate ambassadors of play.

The aims of this book are therefore:

- To help individuals and organizations come to an understanding of and commitment to children learning through play that will be strong enough to support a change in current practice
- To support practitioners in developing a strong philosophy of learning and development through good quality play and to enable them to articulate this philosophy
- To support the development of reflection and informed action in early years classrooms
- To help practitioners understand about play and its role in learning

- To develop practitioners' skills in providing effective learning through play
- To support managers, and those who hope to become managers, in developing their staff and their setting in the use of play

In addressing these aims the book will also support individuals and settings in meeting the requirements of Local Authority quality assurance schemes and more significantly the requirements of the Early Years Foundation Stage Framework (DfES 2007).

The book structure and content

Chapter overview

Understanding how children learn is an essential step in providing good quality play-based learning, and the first four chapters (Part 1) focus on this. Chapter 1 begins by looking at observation as a means to understanding children. It explores why, what and how we observe.

Chapter 2 explains what we know about children's learning and how this helps our understanding of learning through play. It includes a consideration of brain development and learning theory. This is a reference chapter to which we anticipate you will keep returning.

Chapter 3 explores the influence of social and cultural contexts, relationships, stimulation, health, gender, environment and play on the developing child. It looks at the holistic nature of development and how this affects learning and dispositions to learn.

Chapter 4 draws together information from the first three chapters and presents the key ideas that underpin our understanding of effective learning through play in pre-school.

Part 2 begins to focus more sharply on play and its role in pre-school education.

Chapter 5 is central to the book. It presents a case for why play is an effective medium for learning and identifies the key features of good quality play, enabling the reader to understand and plan for play.

Chapter 6 asks you to consider your own context and needs, at team and individual level, by completing an evaluation of the work of your pre-school, your current practice, knowledge and understanding and the impact on children's learning through play. You are introduced to the idea of action planning for improvement.

The next four chapters (Part 3) provide a set of key principles for developing and supporting play in your setting, focusing on the observation, assessment, provision, planning and intervention cycle.

Chapter 7 supports you by looking at how assessment builds from observation, the role of the practitioner, policy development and one method for recording assessments.

Chapter 8 focuses on the physical learning environment and draws from earlier, more theoretical chapters on learning and play. It looks at the organization and provisioning of the indoor and outdoor setting, offers a framework for quality resourcing, considers some aspects of health and safety and introduces planning of provision areas.

Chapter 9 considers how adults can support sustained and meaningful learning in both adult- and child-initiated play.

Chapter 10 looks at what is involved in planning, drawing on what you have learned about effective play provision, adult intervention, monitoring and assessment and how you can ensure each of these aspects takes place in a coordinated way.

In the final two chapters (Part 4) we consider in more detail the management, evaluation and development of quality pre-school provision.

Chapter 11 is aimed at practitioners who have, or anticipate they will have, management responsibilities in a pre-school. It explores the development of adult relationships, team working and management of the observation, assessment, planning, intervention cycle as well as addressing the issue of quality assurance. Some consideration is given to working with parents.

Chapter 12 reconsiders the initial evaluation (Chapter 6) and considers your new position on learning through play. You are introduced to the improvement cycle and personal action planning.

Appendices contain additional frameworks and pro forma, exemplar material, an overview of key research projects you may find interesting and a brief guide to the Early Years Foundation Stage Framework material.

In addition to the core information, each chapter provides related **Professional development activities (PDA)** – see below. Further to these activities, which are written for all practitioners, there are also activities for those more experienced and those who wish to be more analytical and relate their learning to further study: **Further activities**.

Some activities are written for individual completion; others are for completion by the setting's team but where practitioners do not work as part of a team these activities can be easily adapted. Chapters conclude with sections explaining jargon, references and, for those who wish to learn more, further reading.

In the cases where activities suggest you take photographs of children in the setting, please remember to consult and adhere to the setting's policy regarding parental/carer permission.

How to use this book

Each chapter in this book is a discrete unit that can be worked through with the intention of developing a particular aspect of practice, knowledge or understanding. The book as a whole, however, provides a programme to develop thinking and understanding with an emphasis on practical application and self-awareness.

The personal development activities in each chapter will help you to build up your expertise. Most activities have several sections and involve individual research and reflection followed by discussion and reflection as a team. These meetings are valuable opportunities not only to develop ideas at team level but also to allow individuals to articulate and reconsider their own ideas. We suggest that you sometimes work with a colleague as a 'critical friend', that is, someone with whom you can discuss ideas and who will give you honest feedback. Throughout the book you are asked to observe and describe (watch, listen, take notes, identify), reflect (analyse, interpret, draw upon existing knowledge, skills and understanding), act (decide what action to take, when and how) and evaluate (review against certain criteria and provide evidence). In some sections you will be provided with frameworks. These are a set of ideas or guidelines to help you in developing your context.

In order to understand the complexities of learning through play we ask you to choose one particular child (target child) for the focus of your observations, unless otherwise specified. This will enable you to make a more in-depth study to reinforce your knowledge of child development, support you in understanding how a child approaches and solves problems and gain an insight into their interests. Focusing on one child will help you in deciding how best to support their future learning and development.

As you work through the book you should keep a learning journal. There are details of what this might look like below.

The following section describes the nature of the professional development activities included in the book: work-based guidance and activities for groups or individuals (including managers) for developing learning through play.

Professional development activities: tools to support your learning

Personal learning continuum

Table 0.1 Personal learning continuum

1. Audit (initial position) – identify strengths and weaknesses	2. Supported action – reading, activities, reflections and reviews	3. Evaluation against initial audit – review strengths and weaknesses (new position)	4. Personal action plan

Dependence ————————————————————————▶ Independence

The personal learning continuum (Table 0.1) provides a framework for thinking about your own learning journey. It begins by establishing your current position (1) and takes you through acquiring knowledge and skills (2), evaluating strengths and weaknesses (3) to ultimately taking responsibility for your own development (4). Becoming a reflective practitioner is part of this journey.

The continuum centres on your ability to identify which aspects of play provide effective learning experiences, explain why they are effective, recognize emerging patterns in your observations, identifying those aspects of practice that are less effective and preparing you to challenge your own thinking.

By relating practical evidence to reading and research in the field, you will be more able to clarify your thinking and deepen your understanding. This process involves:

- thinking about everyday activities
- reflecting on a specific event, incident or personal experience
- reflecting on your emotional response or the response of others to an incident/event
- reflecting on the conditions and circumstances that may have brought about the incident
- making and analysing connections between incidents and looking for patterns
- interpreting, questioning and re-evaluating
- considering wider cultural and social contexts
- discussing with a 'critical friend' issues and experiences
- relating the understanding of new concepts to previous experiences and knowledge

The outcomes of your reflections may be:

- the resolution of a particular issue
- new learning, a new course of action or reforming of ideas, values and attitudes
- greater self-awareness and the ability to identify your own strengths and weaknesses
- a feeling of empowerment; the confidence and power to take action in your professional development and practice
- recognition of the importance of research in professional development
- improved performance within a team

Although there are no specific learning continuum activities, the process it describes underpins the learning journey you will make. The book will support you on this journey: Chapter 1 will help you to establish your current position (audit); Chapters 2 to 5 and 7 to 11 will help you acquire knowledge and skills (supported actions); Chapter 6 will support you in evaluating strengths and weaknesses (evaluations against initial audit) while Chapter 12 guides you in developing your ideas about further activities (personal action plans).

Personal learning journal

Your personal learning journal may include:

- written observations and completed personal learning journal record sheets (see Table 0.1 for a pro forma)
- thoughts from dialogue with a 'critical friend'
- ideas maps
- photographs
- reflections on resources and materials you have used
- notes from any of the activities in this book
- reflections on group processes

Some journal entries will be made using the personal learning journal record sheet (Table 0.2); here are some key questions to help you complete the sheet.

Observation/Description
- What is it you wish to reflect on and why? (Write a brief description of the issue or observation. Give some contextual and background information. Include your feelings, practical issues, interests and reading.)
- Who was involved? (children/adults)

Reflection
- What have you learned from this experience or incident that will help you in your practice? (Include your interpretations, questions, reflections on your current knowledge, skills and understanding.)
- What other information do you need to gather to help you reflect? (Include different viewpoints, observations and further reading.)
- What questions might you ask your critical friend? (Keep these questions open ended and focused on your incident.)
- How do you feel about what you have learned? (Consider positive and negative responses and emotions.)
- What have you learned about yourself? (Consider your reaction, response, thoughts, current skills, knowledge and understanding. **Be honest and open with yourself**.)

Action
- What action will you take next? (This may include a change of resources, environment, activity or something you will change in yourself.)
- How will you implement and monitor this action?

Evaluation

- What have you learned from your reflection on this incident/experience? (Ask yourself: did I choose the right focus? Did I ask myself the correct questions? Did I take the correct action? What attitudes, expectations, beliefs am I challenging and would change?)
- What will you do to learn more effectively?
- What will you take as your contribution to a team meeting?

Table 0.2 Personal learning journal record sheet

Name:
Date of Reflection:
1. Observation/Description
2. Reflection
3. Action
4. Evaluation

The purpose of the personal learning journal record sheet is to support you in being reflective. It also provides evidence that will support you in articulating:

- your current understanding and perceptions of play and learning in your setting
- dilemmas, concerns and issues to be resolved as an individual and as a setting
- the appropriate kind of action to take
- new knowledge, skills, understanding, concepts and perceptions about play and learning
- personal feelings and thoughts
- your needs for further training

In each chapter you will find personal learning journal boxes. These contain various professional development activities that build on and extend the theme of the chapter. As you complete each of these activities you may be asked to produce evidence of your thinking and actions or prepare material for the team meeting; this work will form the content of your personal learning journal.

Ideas maps

In some of the activities you are asked to create an ideas map, which is simply a spider web or topic plan where you put down all your ideas in a visual format in order to represent and organize knowledge and understanding. See Figure 0.1 for an example of this. You start with a main concept expressed in one key word, short statement or a symbol and from this lines or arrows are drawn to other ideas. Key phrases may be written to identify the connection between the words or statements. Colours may be used to represent each idea and make connections. This method enables you to put down quickly on paper in a memorable format your thoughts on a specific theme. It helps you to sift out key information; it may prompt memories and it can be added to and shared with others at any time.

Figure 0.1 An example of an Ideas Map

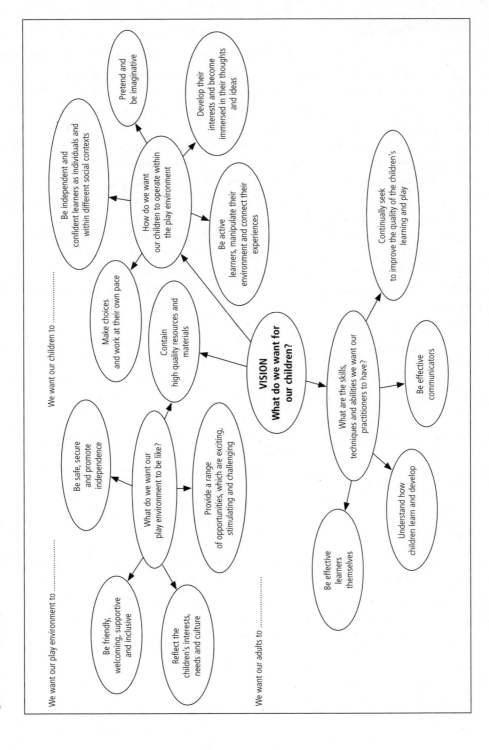

Team meetings

Where a whole setting wishes to develop their practice, i.e. where an organization has decided to follow the programme of activities to improve everyone's practice, then activities and foci for discussion and reflection are included in 'Team Meetings' boxes. Members of a reflective team should listen to each other and engage in dialogue in an informed and responsive manner in order to support their learning. They should collaborate by sharing experiences, responses and reflections in order to solve problems, clarify issues and meaning. By looking at why they do things and the effect it has on others they create a culture in which they can formulate and take ownership of their values and principles for play and learning. By being part of a reflective team each individual is facilitated in articulating his or her understanding and given the confidence to self-improve and implement a change in practice.

We assume the manager/leader is part of the early years team, learning alongside the other practitioners in the setting, and that leadership is not only about systems and procedures but also about working with, and responding to, the needs of practitioners.

In order for team meetings to be effective the following guidelines should be kept in mind:

- Someone must take the lead; this may not necessarily be the manager but should be someone who can keep the team focused and is respected by the team members.
- Everyone should be prepared to make a contribution. Personal learning journals and the activities themselves will help you in making a contribution.
- Opinions, thoughts, suggestions should be listened to, respected and valued.
- Notes should be kept of discussions, agreements and future action. In some cases it will be appropriate to circulate these notes after the meeting.
- There should be some consideration as to how you will keep, store and record the activities and notes for future reference.

Further activities

As mentioned above, these are for those who are more experienced and those who wish to be more analytical and relate their learning to further study.

Starting the journey

Before starting the book we suggest you take some time to think about where you are now as an individual, and where your setting is, in terms of understanding children's learning through play and making good quality provision for such learning. Activities 0.1–0.4 begin this learning process. The notes you make will be reviewed later in the book.

You will need to work on your own and with your team (although if you are not working with a team you can complete the team activities as an individual).

Activity 0.1: Personal learning journal

Purpose: To identify your personal motivation for beginning the book.

Write down in your journal a few ideas under the heading: Why am I reading this book and what do I hope to gain from it?

Activity 0.2: Team meeting

Purpose: To identify your setting's reasons for working together through the book and to consider your team's present understanding of play.

Points for discussion:

- As a team consider what you hope to gain from going through the book together. You do not have to spend a long time on this but you do need to identify three or four of your chief reasons. Note these down wherever you are going to record the team's activities; you will return to these at the end of the book.
- Share with the rest of the team your earliest memory of play and why you think it was so memorable.
- Spend some time now as a team thinking about what you mean by play. Using an ideas map, try to record all you know about play, for example, what counts as play, what qualities it has and how you think play benefits children. This will help you clarify your present understanding as a team and prepare you for the next, individual activity. Now, in another colour, add things you have heard about but do not understand or are not clear about. Keep the map as you will return to it later on in Chapter 5.

Activity 0.3: Personal learning journal

Purpose: To identify your own level of understanding.

- Think in more detail about your knowledge, understanding and practice in relation to play and try to note down things you feel secure about, the things you need clarification about and the things you have heard of but do not understand at all. You might use the following format (Table 0.3), or a copy of the setting's ideas map annotated to show the same information.

Table 0.3 Where am I now in terms of my understanding of play and learning?

I am sure about this	I know about this but need clarification	I have heard of this but do not understand what it means
e.g. How play helps physical development	e.g. The difference between cooperative and collaborative play	e.g. Heuristic play

Activity 0.4: Team meeting

Purpose: To note how play is used in the setting.

As a team consider how the setting provides for play and how your children use the provision in their play. It is enough simply to describe what happens; you can use notes, maps and photographs to record what you do. The following questions may help to guide you but they are only a starting point.

- In what kind of play activities do children get involved?
- When do they play?
- How long do they play in one kind of activity?
- Who decides where and when they play?
- Do they play indoors and outdoors?
- Who decides whom they play with?
- Do you plan for play? If so how and who is involved?
- What is the balance between play and non-play?
- How is the space for play in the setting arranged?
- What kind of resources do children play with?
- Describe one play situation in detail

Note any issues about children's play that emerge from your discussions. For example, 'We don't go outdoors much because we don't have enough staff to cover.'

Further reading

Goodfellow, J. (2004), 'Documenting professional practice through the use of a professional portfolio', *Early Years: An International Journal of Research and Development* 24 (1), March 2004.

References

Broadhead, P. (2004), *Early Years Play and Learning: Developing Social Skills and Cooperation.* London: Routledge Falmer.

DfES (Department for Education and Skills) (2007), *The Early Years Foundation Stage: Setting the Standards for Learning, Development and Care for Children from Birth to Five.* DfES.

Part One
HOW CHILDREN LEARN

The Role of the Adult: Making Observations and Understanding the Child

1

Chapter Outline

Introduction	17
The role of the practitioner as observer in understanding children's play	18
What is observation?	18
Why observe children play?	19
A framework for effective observation	21
Ethics	24
Summary, Jargon explained, Further reading, References	27

Introduction

Effective practitioners continuously develop their knowledge and understanding of the ways in which children develop and learn and use this in order to support and extend children's learning. They therefore have a key role in the process of children learning through play, which includes:

- the provision of an appropriate context – including the physical environment and the ethos created
- the provision and maintenance of resources
- the introduction of new resources to support play development
- supporting play through interaction
- modelling play
- providing social and emotional support to the child
- planning next steps

At various stages during a session the adult is involved in facilitating play, observing children at play, assessing and intervening. This process may be repeated several times and in different time frames.

Purpose of this chapter

This chapter is about observing children in their play and will support you in developing your knowledge, understanding and skills in making observations.

The role of the practitioner as observer in understanding children's play

For practitioners to have a key role in the process of children learning through play they need to understand:

- where the child is in his development
- what the child's current learning concerns are
- how the child is spending his time in various aspects of the play provision
- how they are using the resources and manipulating materials
- how they engage with others and their attitudes to learning

The practitioner must become a skilled observer in order to gain this knowledge: one who listens to what children have to say and watches carefully what they do.

Effective learning takes place when the practitioner starts with the child, addressing those things that interest him.

> The research shows that the more knowledge the adult has of the child the better matched their
> support and the more effective the subsequent learning. Siraj-Blatchford et al. (2002: 48)

What is observation?

Observation is not just looking; it also involves listening and note-taking in an objective manner. We can observe play either formally or informally.

A formal observation is watching and listening to children with the clear intention of studying a particular behaviour or ability, or answering a very specific question. The observation has a focus; it is carried out systematically with the clear intention of understanding children. This includes their behaviour and learning, such as skills and knowledge, interests and thought processes, social interactions and attitudes to learning. It involves note-taking, probably using a particular recording method, and can be a diagnostic tool as it provides information for reflection, analysis and discussion.

Informal observation is also about watching, listening and noticing but in a way that may not be systematic or have a planned focus. The practitioners will become more proficient at informal observation after they have developed their skills in making formal observations. There are things children do or say that are not part of the planned play provision and yet may reflect significant learning or development. Informal observation is about noticing these things, thinking and reflecting on them and making connections. It may involve informal recording: for example, notes on Post-its that allow the practitioner to quickly record the moment; this involves being continually alert and paying attention.

Both forms of observation require the practice and development of observation skills.

Why observe children play?

The main purpose of formal observation, in the educational context, is to understand children and their learning. It also informs planning and intervention by directing the adult's attention to the children's strengths and needs and how they operate within the play environment. Observation allows adults to identify changes in behaviour, ensure appropriate provision and set realistic goals and is part of the assessment, planning and intervention cycle. Figure 1.1 demonstrates how observation and assessment inform planning and practitioner intervention.

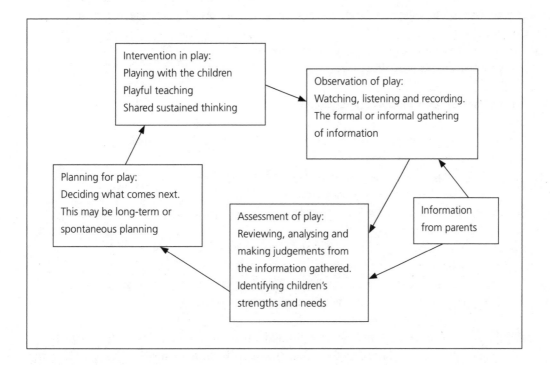

Fig. 1.1 The observation, assessment and intervention cycle

Objective observation provides both a realistic and more accurate view of children's behaviours and events and evidence for informed and reasoned judgements about children's learning. It may even challenge our assumption about what is happening. It also gives feedback on management issues, the effectiveness of resources and the play environment and information about diversity, inequalities, prejudices and stereotyping.

Observation enables the practitioner to:

- decide whether or not to intervene in the children's play
- make decisions about how to support the children's learning, e.g. by adding resources or taking away redundant resources, deciding what questions to ask
- discuss children's learning with other colleagues from an in-depth informed stance
- make sure some children do not dominate a play situation and that more reticent children become involved
- make sure there are enough choices in the play provision for children to extend and make connections in their learning
- pre-empt any problems
- identify opportunities for engaging with a child in sustained shared thinking (see Chapter 9)
- identify opportunities for the children to problem solve, use trial and error, share, collaborate and negotiate
- observe children's routines and patterns in their behaviour
- identify any health and safety issues

Formal observation supports practitioners in:

- embedding the process of observation, reflection and intervention into their practice because formal observations are pre-planned
- developing a systematic approach for using observational information to plan future steps in the children's developmental and learning process
- building up a picture and developing their knowledge and understanding of children's development and learning through play
- analysing, reflecting on and interpreting their observations in order to address any concerns about a child's development in order to make the correct provision
- articulating their understanding of the children's play with parents/carers and other adults
- challenging their own responses, thoughts, assumptions and concerns

Emphasis on observing children in a limited range of activities may allow significant achievements to go unnoticed as the contexts in which children reveal significant learning and understanding are often unexpected and unconventional. We should recognize that every situation is a learning experience and therefore observe children in a variety of contexts, over a period of time, to be sure of the accuracy of our judgements.

Judgements about what children do often underestimate the depth and complexity of their thinking. It is through careful observation and interaction with children that we can get a true picture.

We should seek every opportunity to support children in all aspects of their learning. This may also provide additional and significant information for evaluating play provision.

A framework for effective observation

The following are guidelines, which will help you in improving your observations.

What to look for when observing children's play

Observations will give you information about children's learning through play and about the learning environment. The key things to observe are children's:

- perspectives of their context, e.g. their ideas about play, their play experiences, with whom they like/ dislike to play, feelings, and play routines
- interests, repeated behaviours, routines and patterns, e.g. a particular schema
- responses to both adults and their peers, e.g. the level to which they are able to cooperate or collaborate in their play, the way in which they respond to some aspect of adult support
- attitudes to learning and level of engagement and involvement in a particular play activity, e.g. can they involve themselves in an activity for a sustained period of time and with deep concentration?
- development: perceptual-motor, physical, intellectual, linguistic, emotional or social
- knowledge and understanding of the curriculum; have they acquired a particular skill or concept
- use of resources, e.g. whether a particular resource is being used or not or how well they handle particular materials
- safety, e.g. whether the environment is safe or whether the children are using a particular tool correctly
- interaction with the play environment, e.g. is there enough space for a particular activity, are resources accessible to the children?

Methods of observation

There are a number of methods that can be used for recording observations. Whichever method is chosen, there needs to be some basic information included.

- Date, start and end time
- The number of children and adults involved

- The name/names of children with their dates of birth
- The focus for the observation
- Evaluation and proposals for future action (made after reflection and informed by your knowledge and understanding)

Method 1: Time sampling

- Observations of behaviours taken at set intervals; a note is made of what the child is doing/saying
- Recording method: simple pro forma
- Good for: studying patterns in learning or behaviour over a given period of time; looking at how long the child spends on an activity, to whom the child speaks/listens

Method 2: Event sampling/tallies

- Provides a record of how often a particular behaviour happens over a period of time
- Recording method: simple pro forma, Post-its and photographs
- Good for: building up a picture of one child over a period of time; studying one aspect

Method 3: Checklist

- The observer checks off listed behaviours
- Recording method: simple checklist pro forma
- Good for: identifying strengths and weaknesses; identifying progress against developmental norm or objective; easy to administer

Method 4: Narrative

- Like a diary, an observation written as you observe
- Recording method: diary or notebook
- Good for: recording noteworthy aspects of development or learning, as they occur; allowing for a 'free' approach to writing up; collecting information about all aspects of the event for later analysis

Method 5: Anecdotal records

- The observer records observations of brief instances in a child's behaviour or snippets of language
- Recording method: Post-its and transferred to the permanent record later
- Good for: informal observation and capturing those aspects of learning that occur which are not part of the planned curriculum; recording achievements

Method 6: Visual images

- A visual record (permission must normally be obtained from the parent or carer prior to this method of observation being used)

- Recording method: digital photographs, video recordings
- Good for: capturing a one-off snapshot or observing development or learning over a period of time; useful in conjunction with other methods such as event sampling or anecdotal records; particularly useful for sharing with children; recording children's movement capability

Method 7: Learning stories

- This method came out of the New Zealand Te Whariki Early Years Curriculum Project (Ministry of Education 1996) and the work of Dr Margaret Carr (Carr 2001)
- The observer focuses on the 'can do' by describing really important events, in the form of a story. Different ways in which children learn, their strengths, interests, learning dispositions and progress over a period of time are recorded.
- Recording method: pro forma, digital photographs
- Good for: recording children's learning journeys; embedding in everyday practice; focusing on learning processes and progress; identifying children's interests and approaches to learning as well as skills, knowledge and strategies; describing the relationship between the learner and the environment. They can be a single observation or a series of observations linked together

Developing a strategy for observation and its management

For making formal observations:

- Decide beforehand your focus for observation and the most appropriate method
- Negotiate with your team so that you are free to work
- Collect everything you need, including all the background information, and record this before commencing the observation
- Make sure you are comfortable and can see the child(ren) you are observing
- Try to be inconspicuous; avoid eye contact as this encourages the children to engage with you
- Tell the children you are busy 'watching and listening' and they are to leave you alone
- Note what you see and hear objectively; leave analysis until later
- Avoid making assumptions and using 'labels'
- Do not make comparisons with other children
- Objectively discuss your findings with colleagues

For making informal observations:

- Recognize that everything children do or say whilst in the setting is an opportunity for observation and a step nearer to understanding them
- Be always listening and watching
- Have a system for making quick jottings

- Include these observations with formal observations when analysing, discussing and reviewing children's needs and progress

Ethics

Respect should be shown to those involved in your observations; close observation may be intrusive. Remain objective. This means being aware of, and challenging, subjectivity both as an individual and within group discussion. Be conscious of influences on your thinking and interpretations, such as social and cultural influences, and be aware of the impact of your emotional response on your perceptions and judgements.

Activity 1.1: Personal learning journal

Purpose:

- To practise using a range of observational methods
- To recognize the advantages and disadvantages of each method
- To appreciate the need to choose the appropriate observational method according to what is being observed

Decide upon a set period of time for making a series of observations, e.g. a week.

Every practitioner in the setting practises each method of observation. This is managed so that on any one day each person is using a different method. In preparation for the team meeting you should reflect on the advantages and disadvantages of each method. Use the following questions to help you:

- How easy was the method to use?
- Did it fit in with your daily work?
- Did it give you relevant information?
- Did the method chosen enable you to meet the purpose of your observation?

Activity 1.2: Team meeting

Choose one day from the chosen period and look at the different observation methods used. Compare the information gained from each of the observations. From which method did you learn most about the children observed? Compare how well each method worked across a week, or your chosen period of time.

Consider the following to help you:

- The quality of information gained about the children's learning
- The time taken to use each method
- Practical issues

Decide the method(s) that will fit in best with your way of working.

Further activity

Additionally, the group discusses the following:

- What have you learned about the value of observing play?
- How might you plan observations into the weekly routine of all adults?
- How else will you support practitioner observation?

Activity 1.3: Personal learning journal

Now complete a personal learning journal record sheet (see Table 0.2). In the first section ('Observation/Description') briefly describe Activity 1.1 (above). In the second section ('Reflection') reflect on your implementation of the observation methods, the advantages and disadvantages, analyse your contribution to and the discussion at the team meeting. Consider whether you need to gather other information by reading, talking with colleagues or further experience. In the third section ('Action') identify what action you will take or what you would do differently on another occasion. In the final section ('Evaluation') evaluate what you have learned against the purposes for this activity.

Activity 1.4: Further activity

You are going to carry out a Target Child (Sylva et al. 1980) observation. This has not been explained previously but is another sampling method. It involves choosing a child engaged in some particular aspect of play, writing down what they do and say and with whom at pre-arranged intervals throughout a period of time, e.g. 10 minutes.

Look at Table 1.1, an example of a target child observation record. You will need a watch with a second hand as you are going to record minute by minute as shown in the Time column. Observe for several minutes before you start to record. In the Activity column you will notice the observer has written down exactly what the child does during each minute. In the Dialogue column they have noted what the child says and in the Code column they have indicated to whom with an arrow. They have also noted the Social context, i.e. solitary or collaborative play. Don't forget to include the contextual information on your recording format.

Table 1.1 An example of part of a target child observation record

Time	Activity	Code	Dialogue	Social
1.15	TC hands C2 teddy bear cutter	TC → C2	Here, you try this one	CP
1.16	TC cutting round teddy bear	TC	Mine's called Mary, what's yours?	CP

The codes used are TC – target child, C2 – second child, CP – collaborative play.

Analyse what you have learned about the children's learning from what they say and do. Consider also the advantages for using this method compared with other methods.

This method is useful for efficiently and systematically recording everything that happens. It is therefore particularly useful if you are interested in action research. You should have been able to analyse the skills of the children, their interactions, whether they initiated and led the activity or simply responded, their interests within an activity and levels of concentration and perseverance.

Note down the implications of this method for when and how you observe.

> ### Activity 1.5: Personal learning journal
>
> In addition to the previous entry in your personal learning journal (Activity 1.3) analyse how well you implemented this observation method, what you learned about yourself as a practitioner, your own learning and the learning of the children. Add your analysis to your personal learning record sheet in the Reflection section.

What to do with the information

From making observations you will begin to gather a range of information about the children in your setting. This information should inform discussion about the children's learning, development, interests and experience of play. It will help you in making decisions about play provision. As a setting you will need to decide:

- How will the information be collated and in what format?
- How are the children involved?
- Who contributes and has access?
- When will the information be discussed, at team level and with parents?

One method of dealing with assessment information is to create portfolios, which are collections of significant information regarding the children's learning and development. Each portfolio may contain samples of work, photographs, observations and other relevant material and may be organized chronologically or in areas of learning.

A portfolio allows you to chart the child's progress and provides a resource for discussion with the child, parent, carer and other colleagues. They can be summative and formative.

In order for observations to be a meaningful tool for developing appropriate play provision there needs to be ongoing development of the practitioner's understanding of the play continuum and how children learn. The next chapter looks at the child as a learner and thinker.

Summary

This chapter has highlighted the importance of practitioners being skilled observers in order to understand children's play and learning and to provide appropriate environments and experiences. You have been given a framework for effective observation and have looked at several methods of recording and considered their advantages and disadvantages. This chapter will have prepared you for the further professional development activities in subsequent chapters.

Jargon explained

Action research: a form of practitioner research where individuals enquire, in a systematic way, into some element of their practice with the intention of making improvements on a personal and professional level.

Analysis: looking at your findings in detail in order to understand the child's learning or identify patterns of behaviour and to draw conclusions.

Contextual information: information relating to the context of the observation, such as the setting where the observation took place and the activity, whether another adult was involved, the number, age and gender of children.

Key practitioner: 'The key practitioner makes sure that, within the day-to-day demands of the setting, each child for whom they have special responsibility feels individual, cherished and thought about by someone in particular while they are away from home' (DfES 2007).

Objective observations: simply state the facts and not interpretations.

Further reading

Broadhead, P. (2004), *Early Years Play and Learning: Developing Social Skills and Co-operation*. London: Routledge Falmer.

This book presents us with the Social Play Continuum, a framework or tool for observing children's learning through play. It supports practitioners in understanding the links between intellectual development, language and children's emotional well-being.

Clark, A. and Moss, P. (2001), *Listening to Young Children: The Mosaic Approach*. London: National Children's Bureau and Joseph Rowntree Foundation.

DfES (Department for Education and Skills) (2007), *Statutory Framework for the Early Years Foundation Stage: Setting the Standards for Learning, Development and Care for Children from Birth to Five*. Effective Practice: Key Person.

The Key Person section of this CD-Rom outlines the role and importance of the key person in supporting babies' and young children's learning and development.

Miller. L. (ed.), *The International Journal of Infant Observation and its Applications*.

Available online from Taylor and Francis, the journal publishes writings such as case studies and research papers on young child observations.

Sharman, C., Cross, W. and Vennis, D. (2007), *Observing Children: A Practical Guide*. London: Continuum. 4th edn.

This book is a practical guide to observation techniques. It gives clear instructions on how to make observations and explains why observation is important. It makes use of real observations and case studies.

References

Carr, M. (2001), *Assessment in Early Childhood Settings: Learning Stories*. London: Paul Chapman.

DfES (2007), *Statutory Framework for the Early Years Foundation Stage: Setting the Standards for Learning, Development and Care for Children from Birth to Five*.

Ministry of Education (1996), *Te Whariki: Early Childhood Curriculum*. Wellington, New Zealand: Learning Media Limited.

Siraj-Blatchford, I., Sylva, K., Muttock, S., Gilden, R. and Bell, D. (2002), *Researching Effective Pedagogy in the Early Years* (REPEY). DfES.

Sylva, K.D., Roy, C. and Painter, M. (1980), *Childwatching at Playgroup and Nursery School. Oxford Pre-School Research Project*. London: Grant McIntyre.

The Child as a Thinker and Learner

Chapter Outline

Introduction	30
The brain and learning	31
Children construct their own understanding	33
The role of representation, language and interaction in learning	36
Learning starts from where the child is	41
Scaffolding	42
The spiral curriculum	43
Multiple intelligences	44
Learning dispositions and child involvement	44
Active learning	46
Schema	46
Further study	49
Summary, Further reading, References	49

Introduction

The EPPE (Effective Provision of Pre-school Education Project) research (Sylva et al. 2004), which explored the practice in good or excellent pre-school settings, concluded that one of the factors that determined the quality of a setting was the practitioners' knowledge about how young children learn. They recommended that there should be an improvement in the child development content of both initial and continuing professional development courses.

Understanding about how children learn is an essential step in providing good quality play-based learning. This chapter is about what we know about children's learning; it will explain the key ideas that help our understanding of learning through play. There is a lot to cover, so this is a long chapter. You may find that you will need to tackle it in stages and to return to it as you work through the book in order to revisit key ideas.

Purpose of this chapter

To develop your knowledge and understanding of how children learn.

Before you begin the chapter, complete the following activity. Remember to keep all your notes for future reference.

Activity 2.1: Personal learning journal

Purpose: To help you recall what you already know about learning.

Spend 10 or 15 minutes jotting down all you can remember about how children between the ages of 0 and 5 years learn, perhaps using an ideas map so you can add ideas as you recall them. (You were introduced to ideas maps in the Introduction.)

Keep your work in your personal learning journal.

The brain and learning

The physical health of the brain

We know that the brain develops through use and is fuelled by oxygen and glucose. There is a great deal of evidence that points to the importance of the health and nutrition of the mother to the development of the foetal brain. After birth, the infant's own health and nutrition impact significantly on the development and the functioning of the brain.

How does the brain develop?

Since the development of techniques that allow us to 'watch' the brain working, researchers have discovered more about how it works, although there still remains a lot to learn. When we 'think', electrical and chemical activity occurs within the brain; impulses travel between brain cells (neurons) moving across the gap between individual cells through a synapse (junction). At birth children have only a relatively small proportion of the trillions of synapses established that they will eventually develop, but these connections are sufficient to allow the newborn to survive.

The quality and effectiveness of thinking is not dependent upon the number of brain cells (neurons) we have but rather on how many connections there are between brain cells. The pattern of these connections (neural pathways) is not innate but develops after birth, especially in the time between birth and seven years. The number of connections that have been developed determines the number of pathways within the brain which in turn determines the complexity of the thinking possible for an individual. New connections are added throughout our life and are later strengthened through frequent use or 'pruned' through under-use. Learning is the development of new connections and early childhood is a particularly important period for learning.

We learn different things at different times in our lives. A rapid increase of connections (synaptogenesis), and subsequent pruning of connections, occurs in different areas of the brain at different periods. For example, the area of the brain that processes visual information (visual cortex) develops in the first 12 months and pruning is completed by about 10 years old whereas the part of the brain that deals with complex activities such as planning and decision-making develops later and pruning is not completed until we are about 18 years old (Huttenlocher 1990).

What prompts the changes in the brain?

The young brain develops, and new pathways are established and refined, through the information gathered by the child by means of her own actions and active engagement with the world around her. Experience is crucial in the development of the brain and in its ability to think. Young children's rapid and constant learning is made possible because their brain is different from an adult's; it is more active, more flexible and more sensitive. It is much more affected by experience.

The young brain continues to develop as it meets new forms of stimulation and new experiences. It thrives on variety and stimulation: the richer and more varied the experiences, the more complex the child's neural pathways will be. The brain uses information gathered through all the senses to help it make sense of what it encounters and to build up an internal model of the child's world. 'Everything that a baby sees, smells, hears, tastes and touches, alters the way the brain develops in an increasingly situation-appropriate way' (Riley 2003: 4).

Learning develops through forming and strengthening connections in the brain. New connections are formed with existing mental structures by modifying them and making them more complex. In other words children build on what they already know; this allows them to make sense of the new information and experience.

Emotion and motivation

In a supportive emotional context the child is motivated to learn; emotion is a strong motivator for encouraging the embedding of learning into long-term memory in the brain; some emotions can stop us thinking while others can strengthen an experience so much that we remember it for life. Where learners' emotions are engaged during learning, what they learn is signposted in the brain as important and meaningful and is therefore remembered more readily. 'Emotion is often considered as merely the affective product of learning, but...its role in learning is constructed at a much deeper level. …Emotions shape learning and teaching experiences for both teachers and students' (Ingleton 1999: 9).

Children construct their own understanding

Fundamental to our understanding of children's learning is the concept of the individual as constructor of their own learning (e.g. Piaget 1963), but as we will see later they do not construct alone. Jean Piaget's observations of children led him to the conclusion that humans have an innate desire and ability to learn about the world around them. His observations convinced him that, from birth, children are predisposed to seek to understand the world in which they live, and that they systematically interact with the world around them in order to learn about it. He argued that young children actively seek out the knowledge they need and that they construct their own understandings, learning through first-hand experience by acting on the world. This is very significant in our understanding of learning through play.

Piaget's work on learning revolutionized our understanding of the way children learn, and his ideas have been developed by many other psychologists. Because of the recognition that children construct their own learning, Piaget's school of thought became known as constructivism; a more developed theory grew out of his early work, which is known as social constructivism. Piaget had proposed that the child constructs her learning independently of others but through the work of psychologists such as Lev Vygotsky (1978) and Jerome Bruner (1983), we began to recognize the role of others within the child's society/culture. From this new perspective the child's learning is co-constructed, that is, although the child remains an active learner seeking to make sense of the world, she does so with the help of those around her who are more experienced and knowledgeable. The culture of a child's world, its stories, its ways of doing things, its language, provides the child with 'tools for thinking'. Its explanations help the child to understand what happens around her and to make sense of her experience.

Figure 2.1 Children construct their own understanding through their interaction with the world around them

The child making sense of the world

We understand an experience if it fits with what we 'know'. If it does not make sense to us we are motivated to find out, to learn, to construct a new or altered internal model; in other words to get to 'know'. Children have an innate desire to 'make meaning'; they are motivated to learn by their desire to make sense of the world and by a need to construct a mental model of the world that matches what they experience around them. When what they experience conflicts with what they 'know' they are stimulated to explore further and to build an internal model nearer to reality.

How do children come to understand the world around them?

Children learn about the physical world through spontaneous exploration, play and observation of what is around them. They handle material and find out what it does, they observe the relationship one thing has to another, from birth they observe others and imitate what they do; in this way they come to understand how the physical world works. Understanding the world of ideas, however, is more complex because ideas cannot be experienced directly.

We know that from the earliest onset of language young children talk about experiences. At first this is not about ideas but about how they feel, what they would like and how they see things. They use language to control the world around them, to get the things they need. Later, usually sometime around their second birthday, we see evidence through pretend play that children are developing an understanding of ideas, an understanding of what is real and what is not real, and an ability to create other realities in their minds. At first children can only think about things that they can experience first hand. Using objects to stand for other things, such as a block for a telephone, is the first step towards being able to think about things that they cannot actually see (abstract thinking).

Usually by the child's third birthday, this understanding of 'ideas' begins to develop further through play, and children can be observed trying out their ideas and coming to understand that they can 'know things', they can 'have ideas about things'. This is the onset of metacognition, a growing awareness of their own thinking, an understanding of their own cognitive processes and the ability to consciously apply thinking strategies. However, not for another year or two, when they have developed a 'theory of mind', do they understand that there are things they do not know and that other people might hold different beliefs about things. Developing this 'theory of mind' happens naturally through play and interaction with others, especially their siblings and peers, and at this point play becomes more complex and allows children to explore the ideas of others.

Researchers' own writing is often not very accessible; however, if you wish to read more about Piaget, Vygotsky and Bruner most books on child development outline their work, for example Pound (2005), which provides a straightforward introduction to the work of several key writers.

Figure 2.2 A theory of mind develops through play and interaction with others

The role of representation, language and interaction in learning

Representing their understanding is an essential step in children's learning. Having to re-express (re-present) an idea/concept in a variety of ways requires that they make extensive connections in the brain and reorganize the meaning (semantic network).

Representation embeds the learning more deeply. Most people have had the experience of understanding something more clearly after having represented an event by explaining it to someone else. Children especially need to represent their knowledge and understanding in a variety of ways in order to develop deep learning. All forms of human communication are potential tools for the representation of ideas. Very young children communicate very effectively through movement and sound, and later such things as painting, drawing, singing and dancing are added to their repertoire.

Ways of learning: Modes of representation

Piaget and Bruner were instrumental in raising awareness of the ways in which children learn. However, while Piaget related each mode to a particular period of childhood development, Bruner saw each mode as emerging and dominating each developmental phase, but remaining present and accessible throughout an individual's life. He proposed that there are three modes of learning, which he called enactive (learning through action – manipulating objects, spatial awareness), iconic (learning through seeing – visual recognition and the ability to compare and contrast what is seen) and symbolic (abstract reasoning – learning through symbols such as language). Babies begin their learning in an enactive way, they learn by doing; later they are able to learn through images and finally through verbal and then written language and other symbols. Even as adults we will use all three modes as we learn new things.

1. Enactive learning and representation: The importance of physical movement

> Representation means being able to 're-play' in the mind the 'look' of objects or the movement patterns of objects or the other features of objects that have been experienced. Action or movement 're-play' can be seen when a child uses some simple object (such as a stick) to represent objects moving, such as an aeroplane or a car (Athey 1990: 40).

For many years those who have worked with children have appreciated, through experience, that young children learn through acting physically on the world; early learning is achieved through movement. Observation of very young babies exploring their own bodies and the things within their reach, young children exploring the contents of the kitchen cupboard or treasure baskets, and older children constructing with blocks, have all revealed the same learning behaviour. Young children learn to move and move to learn. This period of intense learning through physical action is crucial to later learning as it establishes cognitive structures that will form part of later more complex understandings.

2. Iconic learning and representation: The importance of context and image

In the second mode of learning and remembering, the child represents the world through images and spatial schemas – images can now stand for objects and the child's model of the world is stored as visual images. Children begin understanding what images represent; they are able to represent things themselves in iconic form. 'Children's drawings are an attempt to communicate a narrative and to explain the meanings that the children have in their minds' (Van Oers, undated).

3. Symbolic learning and representation: Going beyond the information given

At this point children can encode their experience of the world symbolically, to represent ideas and things in a way that is not a direct literal representation of the form and appearance of the thing itself. It allows them to think about things without the thing being present or bringing its appearance to mind; this allows children to think abstractly, to think about 'what if'. Language plays the major part in this process.

Children learn concepts by going through the three modes of learning; first by manipulating the objects, then by representing them iconically and finally by representing the idea of the object symbolically.

Figure 2.3 Children develop their understanding through representing their experiences symbolically

The role of language in the development of thinking

Language has a particularly important role in learning. Language acts to describe, explain and encapsulate our culture for each new generation.

> Language objectifies reality and makes possible the transmission of meaning (and its evaluation) across generations who share common concepts (Bruner and Haste 1987: 5).

The language of any culture serves to describe that culture, its ways of seeing and its ways of doing. Children learn through and with others and in this process the role of language is crucial. Children need language in order to think, to represent their understanding; language is a 'tool of the mind'. The words and structure of the language children use influence the way they perceive their environment. In this way, according to Vygotsky, ways of thinking are determined by culture, just as the tools you are given for any everyday task will influence the way you tackle the task and the results you get. The tools you have reflect the things you need to do and the things you value; the language a culture develops represents the ideas they need to communicate and the things they value.

Through interaction with others, children build up more complex models of the world, they do not have to learn everything from scratch and without support; they can use what others say and do to help them build their understanding. The words they learn and come to understand carry meaning given to them by their own culture; the words encode complex meanings that allow children to share their thoughts, understanding and values.

> Through language, the child is quickly aided into her entry into culture: its metaphors, its kinds of explanations, its categories, and its ways of interpreting and evaluating events. These are not invented by the child; they are the common currency of the culture, the framework that determines the boundaries of the child's concepts (Bruner and Haste 1987: 2).

The importance of children's own talk in learning

Although closely related to the previous section we look at children's own talk separately because in the early years of learning its importance is well established. In 1967 the Plowden Report lent powerful support to the idea that children's talk was a central mechanism in their learning:

> Spoken language plays a central role in learning...Through language children can transform their active questioning response to the environment into a more precise form and learn to manipulate it more economically and effectively...Language increasingly serves as a means of organising and controlling experience and the child's own responses to it (DES 1967: Part 2, p. 19, para. 54).

The young child uses egocentric speech, i.e. talk to and for themselves; it is the constant talk you hear with young children as they describe to themselves what they are doing or what they are going to do. The function of this talk is to control their own actions; it is essential to their learning process, it is thinking out loud. As the child develops, this becomes inner speech, or thought, but egocentric speech does not entirely disappear; even adults at times when they are challenged by a task will revert to thinking out loud. Even after egocentric speech becomes thought, children still need opportunities to express their thoughts out loud; this allows them to re-present their ideas to themselves, to evaluate them, to re-form them, to make connections with other ideas and to embed them more securely in their memories.

> People need to talk. Take talking away from them and you deprive them of something valuable, take talking away from children and the process of education grinds to a halt. We must make space – a large space – in the curriculum where the need of a child to talk is recognized and encouraged (Reed 1983: 120).

How do young children learn to use language?

Children are born into a world of complex symbolic representation, such as spoken language, which they must master in order to function effectively in their culture. The brain seems inclined to listen to and try to make sense of the sounds it hears, and to understand what they mean.

Children learn to use language by hearing others talk. At birth babies are able to distinguish between all human speech sounds but the brain seeks out the sounds it hears in its environment and 'forgets' those it does not; in this way the young child concentrates on the sounds it will need for the language of its own culture. At about a year old, children move from sounds to words and begin to associate words with objects, using their experience of the words they hear those around them use. Normally before their second birthday most children have learned around 20 to 50 single 'label' words but they need also to understand the sense of a word and the relationship it has with practical activity.

> The understanding of the relationship between sign and meaning that dawns on a child at this point (between 1½ and 2yrs) is something different in principle from sound images and object images and their association (Stern 1914: 109-10).

By about 18 months children begin to make the connection between meaning and language, and once they come to understand that words have meaning the speed at which they learn new words accelerates so that by the time they are five, most have acquired a vocabulary of 5,000 words or more. Throughout childhood individuals continue to learn new words at an enormous speed through interaction with more knowledgeable individuals.

How the words they are learning are used in combination forms the grammar of a culture's language and this is the next linguistic skill children must acquire to make themselves understood. How this occurs is an excellent example of how children strive to make meaning rather than just imitate what they see and hear. At first children do seem merely to imitate the language structures they hear. At about two years old they tend correctly to say 'went' and 'sheep' but increasingly they construct a 'theory of grammar' for themselves based on what they know. For example, a common error for three-year-olds is to form the past tense of all words using the commonly used 'ed', for example, go-ed or went-ed instead of went, and the plural of all words using 's', for example, 'sheeps'. Rather than being errors, these words can be seen as evidence of the child trying to make sense of complex rules that have not yet been taught to them. Such errors suggest that, before two, children copy words they hear from more experienced language users, but later, having worked out and internalized the rules about language they apply them in a generalized manner, sometimes incorrectly.

Meta-language: Talking about ideas and knowledge

At home the child gradually learns the language of the home culture and what it means, just as they learn the rules and ways of doing things. Starting nursery or school, however, drops the young child into a 'new language' environment. This place is different from home; the language the adults use is different. For those children who come from cultural backgrounds different from the adults this difference can be enormous; but for every child there will be differences, e.g. 'circle time', 'line-up', 'home corner' are phrases they are unlikely to come across at home.

> With younger children much research [...] has shown that the unfamiliar language of the school can inhibit the child's normal communicative competence and performance, and so it is important to allow opportunities for sharing intentions from verbal instructions as often as possible (Moyles 1992: 91).

Of particular interest to the practitioner, then, is the need for children to learn the new language and what it means in different contexts. This is also true of the language associated with different areas of learning. For example, the word 'ball', when used during outdoor play, is unlikely to mean the same as it does in the story of Cinderella. In mathematics, we often use words very differently from the way we use them in everyday life and this can cause problems for children's understanding, for example, when we talk about big numbers when big is normally used to refer to physical size. Children learn all these complex meanings and relationships through interaction with others and through trying the words for themselves.

Learning starts from where the child is

As with any construction, children build their learning from the base. They build on what they already know, that is, their present level of development. Learning occurs in the area just beyond what the child already knows. This is the area of mental functions currently in an embryonic state; these functions are in the process of maturation. Within this area we learn with the aid of others. The term coined by Vygotsky (1978) to describe this area was the zone of proximal development (ZPD) which he defined as:

> ...the distance between the actual development level as determined by independent problem solving and the level of potential development as determined through problem solving under adult guidance or in collaboration with more capable peers (Vygotsky 1978: 86).

In any area of learning there are things that children know and can do well enough to function unaided but there is a higher level (assisted competence) they can achieve with the support of a more knowledgeable peer or an adult – it is the area between these two that Vygotsky called the zone of proximal development.

When young children have the skills to put one brick on top of another but cannot yet build a tower of bricks the adult holds the lower bricks to steady the structure; when they can pedal and steer a bicycle but have not yet learned to balance, the adult holds onto the seat, or fits stabilizers to assist balance; when they can say numbers in order and understand about cardinality but have not quite grasped the principle of one-to-one correspondence, the adult counts with them to match the rate of the child's pointing to each object. In these instances we see 'assisted competence'. We see activity that, with support 'today', children will be able to do by themselves 'tomorrow'.

Vygotsky saw it as the role of the educator to offer challenges that fall within the ZPD so that whilst it was just beyond what the child could do alone it was still achievable with assistance and would result in learning. Vygotsky argued that the most effective teaching is aimed at the higher level of the child's ZPD. However, to go beyond the ZPD will, as a rule, result in the child ignoring, not using, or incorrectly using those skills that fall outside of her ZPD. Berk and Winsler (1995) call this 'a dynamic zone of sensitivity'.

Scaffolding

The idea of scaffolding grew out of the concept of the ZPD. Bruner (1966) developed the concept of assisted performance, which he called scaffolding, by looking in more detail at how experts can support a novice's learning. In his work Bruner stresses the role of the adult or more able peer in helping the child to make sense of the experience. He felt that the most fruitful experience in a child's education was her collaboration with more skilled partners. The more experienced partner provides help in the way of an intellectual scaffold, which allows the less experienced learner to accomplish more complex tasks than may be possible alone.

In essence the idea of the interaction between the novice and the expert as 'scaffolding' for the child's thinking is seen to act first in supporting the learning and second in providing assistance to the child in her attempts to represent her understanding. The degree of support given is determined by the learner's need; it enables the child's achievement but was then gradually dismantled and withdrawn when the support is no longer required. Both the building and the dismantling of the support require a skilful and sensitive adult.

Scaffolding may take the form of verbal or non-verbal interaction, which includes the introduction of resources and the modelling of action. Although verbal language is the mode many educators identify with scaffolding, other strategies such as play, objects and gesture can be used very effectively. Key approaches might involve engaging the child in an interesting and meaningful problem-solving activity, focusing the child's thinking, encouraging and supporting the child until she becomes self-motivated and managing, drawing the child's attention to critical features of a problem, demonstrating and allowing the child to imitate the behaviour and assisting recall. All these things can be done using a multitude of strategies; in Chapter 9 we will explore some of them.

Scaffolding also provides children with support in using the forms of representation adopted by their culture; it helps them express ideas in words, in drawing, in movement, in number, in music, in painting and so on. They learn, for instance, to use words and numbers to express ideas of time, to use drawing to represent events and objects.

> The child learns to understand these 'representations and symbols of culture' through using them within a supportive framework provided by adults and peers (Bruner and Haste 1987: 163).

More recent work has emphasized the need to establish an equal partnership between novice and expert, with an emphasis on mutuality; scaffolding relies more on guided participation, instructional conversation, cooperative learning and sustained shared thinking, which will be discussed in Chapter 9.

The spiral curriculum

Jerome Bruner (1960) proposed that concepts no matter how complex begin their development in some simple form. His observations of children learning led him to identify what he called the spiral curriculum. He claimed that any concept is first learned in some simple form by children; it is then returned to in increasingly difficult and more formal forms as the individual develops. The image of a spiral curriculum is a way of expressing this; a skill or an idea is developed throughout our lives by making connections with other knowledge and revisiting the skill or concept at a progressively higher and more abstract level. The idea that begins as a baby's fascination with dropping toys from the highchair ends with complex ideas of gravity which form part of the physics curriculum.

The concept of the spiral curriculum highlights the importance of the children's first-hand experience in the early years and the importance of their explorations of relationships between ideas rather than just mastering facts.

> A curriculum as it develops should revisit these basic ideas repeatedly, building upon them until the student has grasped the full formal apparatus that goes with them (Bruner 1960: 13).

The implication of the spiral curriculum is that children can be exposed to quite difficult ideas and skills through appropriate experiences matched to their present intellectual abilities. It might also suggest that we think carefully about how the experiences we offer might help children begin to build their later understanding. For example, although the idea of teaching three-year-olds how to do written calculations seems ill advised, very young children have a concept of quantity; just ask them which of two unequal piles of sweets they would like. They can also count, although it is clear that in early stages this is little more than the repetition of words in a learned order, a little like a nursery rhyme. Many children at this stage are also very skilled at sharing things out and other everyday mathematical problems as long as the task is meaningful and concrete. Children learn about mathematical ideas by using them in situations that they understand. It is these experiences that are built upon towards the end of key stage 1 when rather more complex concepts such as division are taught.

Multiple intelligences

For many years it has been recognized that individuals are better at some things than they are at others; that one person is better at some things than is her neighbour. However, it has been an individual's ability with linguistic, mathematical and logical tasks that has been used to measure his intelligence. Although not without critics, who claim for instance that Gardner's choice of intelligences is flawed, the work of Howard Gardner has changed the way we view intelligence. He proposes that although we all have a general intelligence we also have particular intelligences: areas in which we perform particularly well. He identifies eight areas or intelligences: Linguistic, Logical-Mathematic, Spatial, Musical, Bodily-Kinesthetic, Intrapersonal, Interpersonal and Naturalistic Intelligence. If you would like to read more about these see Gardner (1993). The message that early years professionals should take from this work is clear: children need opportunities to learn through and about all these areas of human intelligence, and to represent their learning in a multitude of ways. Learning in all areas needs to be valued and encouraged; over-emphasis on a few areas disadvantages some children and impoverishes the experience of all.

Learning dispositions and child involvement

To be successful learners, individuals need to develop positive learning dispositions; throughout our lives our learning dispositions influence our experience of learning. These dispositions are not the same as learning skills; they are attitudes, approaches, and habits of mind. Claxton (2006b) identifies what he calls the Four Rs of learning power. **Resilience** related to things such as perseverance, relishing a challenge and absorption; **reflectiveness**; **resourcefulness** related to such things as questioning and reasoning; and **reciprocity** related to such things as imitation, empathy and collaboration.

Figure 2.4 Learning dispositions such as concentration and perseverance emerge from children's experience as learners

As Claxton (2006a) points out, having a skill does not mean you are disposed to use it; learning how to use questions, for instance, is of no use if under different circumstances you are not disposed to ask them. How the child's teachers and carers respond to the child and how enabling they are directly affects the development of positive learning dispositions. Dispositions are linked to feelings about ourselves and to our identity and just like our emotional responses the reaction of those significant others around us affects and models our dispositions. For example, in relation to questioning:

> … expanding the capacity to learn means creating a climate in which that feeling of enfranchisement and entitlement is systematically broadened and strengthened – not weakened, undermined or simply ignored. In such a climate, students' questions are welcomed, discussed and refined, so the disposition to question becomes more and more robust; more and more evident across different domains; and more and more sophisticated (Claxton 2006a: 7).

Learning dispositions emerge from children's experience as learners, the learning climate in which they have lived and their own growing sense of themselves as learners. Positive dispositions lead to greater child involvement in activities characterized by such things as high levels of concentration, persistence, motivation and intensity of experience. Laevers (undated) points out the close relationship between well-being and involvement:

> Involvement and well-being are closely linked. This is in fact logical: a child who feels emotionally uncomfortable in class, or who is unhappy, will find it more difficult to take up an activity, and even more so, to become involved in it (Laevers undated: 41).

Involvement is also linked to the level of challenge the activity offers. 'Involvement only occurs somewhere between "being able to do something" and "not yet being able to do something"; "understanding something" and "being on the verge of understanding"' (ibid.: 20). Most productive learning, claims Laevers, occurs when we are so involved with some activity that 'we lose ourselves in it'. The involved child is motivated and gaining an intense learning experience.

The idea of involvement can be seen to draw on the idea of ZPD. Two ideas that seem to unite many of the learning theories we have looked at are the concepts of active learning and of schema.

Active learning

The underlying principle of active learning is the belief that the construction of knowledge is a dynamic process that requires the active engagement of the learner. Early years approaches, such as that which is seen in High/Scope settings, are underpinned by the idea of active learning; of children as the agents of their own learning who are constantly motivated to explore and investigate the world around them in order to make sense of it, to build their own knowledge and understanding of how it works and to represent that learning; of the adult supporting the children in their endeavours and a physical and social environment designed to support learning.

From this well-supported perspective, in order to learn effectively children must be provided with the opportunity to act on and explore the world using all their senses, to have control over how they explore, act and represent that learning.

Schema

In her book *Extending Thought in Young Children*, Chris Athey (1990) writes about the findings of a longitudinal study at the Froebal Institute. During this work she made an interesting discovery about the way in which children direct their own behaviours towards making sense of the world, to construct their understanding of particular concepts. What Athey observed were patterns of repeatable behaviours; she called these behaviours schemas.

A schema is defined both as a pattern of actions (what we do) and a mental structure; these two are linked. As Piagetian theory suggests, 'Our actions depend on what we know and what we know depends on our actions' (McDougall 1986). Athey's action schemas are the 'themes' that can be recognized in children's learning behaviour. Seemingly unrelated play responses may actually be linked by a common thread and represent the child's attempts to understand a concept, to construct an accurate mental model. Children also notice things in the environment or show a particular interest in things that fit in with their current schema. Recognizing these threads can help adults gain access to children's current intellectual concerns to identify what they are trying to learn. During one period of time, for example, a child may begin by climbing in and out of enveloping spaces and when she plays outside she surrounds a space with building crates and takes objects and herself into it. She may also start her block construction by building a surround which she then fills with things. When she paints, the paintings are concerned with representing objects inside other objects or they may be painted over, the act of putting the object in the painting 'inside'. This containing and enveloping schema is very common with pre-school children and seems to signal a desire to understand inside and outside, fullness and emptiness.

The development of schema

Although we may miss some stages in the development of a particular schema, children seem to develop schema first through gross motor play and play with objects; then in symbolic forms such as role play and drawing. These stages mirror Bruner's modes of learning. Schemas do not seem determined by the environment; rather they are fed by it. In other words the child is motivated by a desire to understand an idea and to do this she performs the (action) schema in different contexts in the environment to elaborate or refine her (mental) schema. A child's dominant schema seems to some extent to prescribe how she will react to the environment, what she will find interesting and what she will perceive.

Schemas give us a window into the child's thinking, which we can use to match our interaction and provision more closely to her needs.

> I was watching a child who was spinning his pencil on the table with a twist of his finger. I said, 'You're making it go round aren't you?' Immediately he looked at me with interest, I mentioned some of the things I had seen going round, such as wheels and a cement mixer, and used the word 'rotate'. Excitedly he added things he knew. Once you show in your conversation with a child that you've cottoned on to his current schema, you're his friend for life (Chris Athey cited in McDougall 1986).

Another common schema in pre-school is connection. During this time you might observe: an interest in games where children join hands; objects tied in strings; material stuck together;

drawings and paintings of linked parts; particular interest in stories such as 'The Enormous Turnip' (traditional tale) or 'Funny Bones' (Alhberg, 1980).

Some schemas join to form more complex ones, for example, vertical and horizontal lead to the very common grids found in the patterns of behaviour of five-year-olds.

Activity 2.2: Personal learning journal

Purpose: To identify what your target child is learning in his or her play and what modes of learning they are using.

- During the course of a week take photographs of your target child at play
- Make brief anecdotal notes for each photograph
- Note the learning indicated by your observation in terms of what the children were learning and how they were learning – remember to think about your reasons for your judgement, that is, your evidence
- Finally think about and note what things influenced that learning

Further activity

Write brief notes of which theories throw light on what you have observed.

Identify how what you have seen relates to what you have read in this chapter.

Activity 2.3: Team meeting

Preparation

Prepare a brief summary to support an oral report about your chosen child as a learner.

Meeting

Each member, using the material gathered, should talk to the rest of the group about their child as a learner at play.

Further activity

Note any theoretical issues you think are important and would like to discuss at the team meeting.

Each member of the group should identify one key aspect of theory and give any examples they have observed that illustrate the aspect. The group should then discuss any issues about which members of the group are still unclear.

If you are working alone, study a second child and compare your findings. What do you notice? What similarities are there and what differences?

Activity 2.4: Further activities

- Take each key aspect covered in the chapter and note any examples you have observed that illustrate the aspect.
- Take some time to return to your ideas map from Activity 2.1; add in another colour any new knowledge you have acquired.

Remember to add your work to your learning journal.

Further Study

Identify and record areas you would like to know more about. Follow this through with independent reading. Try to think about how theory can help you understand an area of learning. Here is an example of how theory can help us understand children's learning and mathematical development (number). We can draw on several theories when considering the child's development of number, in particular Piaget's concepts of active learning, Bruner's spiral curriculum and Vygotsky's role of language in learning. Children's early ability to add and subtract objects is based on their first-hand experience with objects (Piaget); it is an ability that will underpin the more formal, abstract type of addition and subtraction they will learn later (spiral curriculum). Between the ages of three and four children can perform well in tasks that involve simple addition and subtraction, if the tasks involve small quantities of objects in contexts with which they are familiar and especially if the task is of their own making (making meaning). For example, 'How many cups do we need for our picnic altogether? We have four people but the baby needs a bottle.' Where the task becomes abstract or meaningless to children they struggle, for example, 'four subtract one' (Piaget's stages/Bruner's modes of learning). Hughes (1986) suggests that this 'stems from a failure to understand a new kind of language, the language of mathematics' (Vygotsky, meta-language and the role of language and learning).

Summary

This chapter should have not only raised your awareness of the complexity of young children's learning but also the very strong and clear implications for early years professionals that emerge from the research we have looked at. Beginning with the research on the brain and its development we will summarize by considering other implications for practice.

We know that:

- The good health and nutrition of mothers and children is essential for children's intellectual as well as their all-round development and so work with mothers before and after the birth of their child is important

- Throughout the early years a child's brain undergoes enormous change; the child learns quickly and constantly and so we should recognize what a crucial time this is for the individual and endeavour to support this learning

- Brain studies show that children develop their understanding of the world best in a situation where they are socially and emotionally well supported so that, although this chapter looks at cognitive development as a separate area, it cannot be separated from a consideration of other areas of development, especially social and emotional development. This has implications for the ethos of the setting and the principles that underpin its practice. Those who seek to educate young children must take account of children's physical health, emotional well-being including their sense of self, their social skills and their ability to get on with others; this will be explored in the next chapter

- The quality and variety of the child's experience affects development; the more multi-sensory input children receive the more secure their learning will be. This indicates that settings should think carefully and creatively about the range of sensory experience available for the child; they should provide opportunities for children to look, listen, touch, taste, move and smell. Children need opportunities to learn in different ways

- The child is an active learner and so early years settings need to give children autonomy in their learning, provide a quality learning context that offers children the 'tools for thinking' and adults who support their learning. Settings need to plan their provision in such a way that children can make genuine choices within a real and stimulating environment; the adults in the setting need to be skilled in their interaction and knowledgeable about learning and about the children in their care

- The concept of the ZPD, the spiral curriculum and scaffolding taken as a whole provides a perspective on children's learning that requires practitioners to broaden ideas of developmental appropriateness, beyond looking only at what the child can do unaided, to include those things the child can do with assistance. From this perspective educators will not wait until behaviours emerge spontaneously before providing activities that encourage their development, for to do so would result in the children working at the lowest level of their ZPD

- Through observation of the children's learning behaviours and action schema, practitioners can judge if the experiences they offer are appropriate for the children's level of development and engage their interest. Where practitioners plan provision based on the careful noting of which kinds of activities support a child's learning, opportunities provided in the setting are more likely to lead to learning

- To learn effectively children need opportunities to re-present their learning in many different forms; settings need to provide opportunities for this to happen

- Spoken language is an important part of learning; children need lots of opportunities to talk and to listen, to themselves and to others. Adults need to engage children in conversation

Figure 2.5 Spoken language is important, children need lots of opportunities to talk and listen

Amongst the most important messages coming from the work of developmental psychologists is that children's main learning achievements, across all domains, come from their own experiences in the course of activities such as play and the exploration, everyday talk and social interaction involved in that play.

> Children's later school success appears to be enhanced by more active, child-initiated learning experiences. Their long-term progress may be slowed by overly academic preschool experiences that introduce formalized learning experiences too early for most children's developmental status. Pushing children too soon may actually backfire when children move into the later elementary school grades and are required to think more independently and take on greater responsibility for their own learning process (Marcon 2002).

Further reading

Schema

Athey, C. (1990), *Extending Thought in Young Children*. London: Paul Chapman.

This is the full research report from the project and would be useful for those who wish to go on to academic study of schema. A more readable book is Nutbrown, C. (1994), *Threads of Thinking* (Paul Chapman), which discusses the application of Athey's work to the classroom.

Representation

An interesting book about children and their drawing is Anning, A. and Ring, K. (2004), *Making Sense of Children's Drawings*. Open University Press (UK).

Learning dispositions

There is now a good range of material on learning dispositions but a good starting point would be Carr, M. (2001), *Assessment in Early Childhood Settings: Learning Stories*. London: Paul Chapman. This book explores Carr's work in New Zealand on developing learning stories. She proposes five domains of learning dispositions:

- taking an interest
- being involved
- persisting with difficulty or uncertainty
- communicating with others
- taking responsibility

and analyses the domains in three parts: being ready; being willing; and being able.

References

Ahlberg, A. and J. (1980), *Funny Bones*. London: Heinemann.

Athey, C. (1990), *Extending thought in Young Children*. London: Paul Chapman.

Berk, L. and Winsler, A (1995), *Scaffolding Children's Learning: Vygotsky and Early Childhood Education*. Washington: National Association for Education of Young Children.

Bruner, J. (1960), *The Process of Education*. Cambridge, Mass.: Harvard University Press.

—— (1966), *Toward a Theory of Instruction*. New York: WW Norton.

—— (1983), *Child's Talk: Learning to Use Language*. Oxford: Oxford University Press.

Bruner, J. and Haste, H. (1987), *Making Sense: The Child's Construction of the World*. London: Methuen.

Claxton, C. (2006a), 'Expanding the capacity to learn: A new end for education?'. Paper to the British Educational Research Association Annual Conference Warwick University. Available from http://www.guyclaxton.com/documents/New/BERA%20Keynote%20Final.pdf (accessed February 2007).

—— (2006b), 'Building learning power'. *Primary Leadership*, Paper 19 (November).

DES (Department of Education and Science) (1967), *Children and their Primary Scho*
HMSO.

Gardner, H. (1993), *Frames of Mind: The Theory of Multiple Intelligences*. London: Fon

Hughes, M. (1986), *Children and Number*. Oxford: Blackwell.

Huttenlocher, P. (1990), 'Morphometric studies of human cerebral cortex development'. *N*
28 (6), 517-27. Available from http://www.ncbi.nlm.nih.gov/sites/entrez

Ingleton, C. (1999), 'Emotion in learning: a neglected dynamic'. Paper from HERDSA Annua ......nal
Conference, Melbourne, 12-15 July 1999. http://www.herdsa.org.au/branches/vic/Cornerstones/pdf/
Ingleton.PDF.

Laevers, F., Vandenbussche, E., Kog, M. and Depondt, L. (no date), *A Process-orientated Child Monitoring
System for Young Children*. Centre for Experimental Education.

Marcon, R. (2002), 'Moving up the grades: Relationship between preschool model and later school
success'. *Early Childhood Research and Practice* 4 (1), (Spring 2002). Available from http://ecrp.uiuc.
edu/v4n1/index.html

McDougall, B. (1986), *Rumpus Schema Extra*. Cleveland: LEA.

Moyles, J. (1992), *Organising for Learning in the Primary Classroom: A Balanced Approach to Classroom
Management*. Buckingham: Open University Press.

Piaget, J. (1963), *The Origins of Intelligence in Children*. New York: Norton.

Pound, L. (2005), *How Children Learn: From Montessori to Vygotsky*. Step Forward Publishing.

Van Oers, B. 'On the narrative nature of young children's iconic representations: some evidence and
implications'. Available from http://psych.hanover.edu/vygotsky/vanoers.html (accessed April 2007).

Reed, R. (1983), *Talking with Children*. Arden Press.

Riley, J. (2003), *Learning in the Early Years*. London: Paul Chapman.

Stern (1914) cited in Vygotsky (1986), *Thought and Language*. Cambridge, Mass.: MIT Press.

Sylva, K., Melhuish, E., Sammons, P., Siraj-Blatchford, I. and Taggart, B. (2004), *The Effective Provision of
Pre-School Education Project*. DfES.

Vygotsky, L. (1986), *Mind in Society: The Development of Higher Psychological Processes*. Cambridge,
Mass.: Harvard University Press.

Aspects of Development Influences on Learning

3

Chapter Outline

Introduction   54

The influence of social and cultural contexts in which the child is
    developing   55

The influences on development: relationships, stimulation, health,
    gender, environment and play   56

How development affects learning and dispositions to learning   61

Play and its influence on children's learning   63

Summary, Jargon explained, Further reading, References   67

Introduction

Young children are continually changing and developing within a variety of social and cultural contexts. This chapter will explore some of the social and cultural influences upon development, the holistic nature of development and how this affects learning.

Purpose of this chapter

To help you understand:

- the factors that may influence the development of the child
- the holistic nature of development and how it may influence learning
- the importance of play in development and the influence of play on children's learning

Activity 3.1: Personal learning journal

Purpose: To raise your awareness of the need to take factors influencing a child's development into account when planning experiences and the play environment.

Before you begin the chapter, think about the children in your setting and consider what influences on development your setting takes into account when organizing play experiences and the environment. For example, a child is finding it difficult to cope with a new baby in the family, so you set up the role-play area in a way that helps her explore the issue. In this case, family changes are recognized as influencing the development of children in your setting.

Activity 3.2: Team meeting

Create an ideas map together of your shared thoughts, about the changing, developing child. You will return to your ideas map at the end of the chapter.

The influence of social and cultural contexts in which the child is developing

According to Vygotsky, learning is shaped by activities that take place in the social and cultural contexts in which we grow up. Children are therefore developing within a series of immediate, influencing contexts, such as their families and homes, the nursery or toddler groups, their peers and friends. These contexts will vary socially and culturally, each having its different rules and expectations. Children will experience their culture through artefacts, images, music, books, beliefs, events, places and people. By being part of various groups, children come to understand there are many ways of doing things in different circumstances.

The context in which the child moves will have different levels of importance and greater meaning depending upon the child's stage in life. Bronfenbrenner (1979) refers to these contexts as the 'microsystem' or 'immediate world of the child' and the 'mesosystem' or 'interrelations' between the groups within the microsystem. Bronfenbrenner also suggests there are indirect contexts or settings (exosystem), which also have an influence. Contexts may be perceived as a positive influence for one child but negative for another. For example, the 'microsystem' of the home has significant meaning and therefore the initial experience of another 'microsystem', such as the first few days of nursery, may be distressing. The impact of this negative experience may be lessened through parents and school working together in supporting the child. The inter-relationship or 'mesosystem' between contexts is therefore important. Indirect influences may also affect the child. For example, father's company (exosystem) decides to relocate, resulting in more travelling and a change of routine for the family and the child. This change for the company may have been triggered by something in the 'macrosystem', such as government policy.

The child's ability to adapt and manage change will have a positive or negative impact upon her development.

The influences on development: relationships, stimulation, health, gender, environment and play

Relationships

Relationships and social emotional development

The influence of adults is important in the social and emotional development of children who, by interpreting their perceptions of how others view them, build up an image of themselves. From the beginning children are greatly influenced by their parents or carers, looking to them for feedback and response. The interpretation of signals between the two is the foundation for future interactions. Through a strong attachment children explore physical differences and emotional reactions. They develop an understanding of love, affection and emotion. Once they recognize and understand that emotions and feelings have meaning and convey information then they can begin to manage them. For example, smiles and cheerfulness display happiness and the message that your presence gives pleasure. Through positive relationships children develop a sense of identity, who they are, where they come from and their place within the family and community. In addition they develop an awareness of their body, feelings and thoughts. Secure relationships, where the adult responds positively, enable children to like and respect themselves and thus develop a positive self-image.

We all create for ourselves a model of an ideal self. Self-esteem is the measure of how we see ourselves in comparison to this ideal model. A smaller distance between the two creates a higher self-esteem. The way in which other people react to us and make us feel also influences our self-esteem. High self-esteem leads to a positive self-concept.

Relationships within the culture influence the way children think, feel, develop ideas and relate to others and is crucial in determining positive self-concept. A secure relationship enables children to develop a sense of trust and security and an awareness of emotion; they will feel supported and are therefore given the opportunity to flourish. A child with poor self-concept may lack persistence, perseverance and the confidence to take part. Making choices and decisions may be difficult. They may show little respect for resources, possessions and other people, have difficulty in learning and accepting rules and constantly test boundaries. Being unable to recognize and control their emotions may lead to conflict.

Relationships and language development

The quality of early interactions will influence language development as this begins with children developing personal communication signs and sounds. They do this with adults and those close to them. They respond to eye contact and facial expressions and later learn to recognize language patterns through hearing familiar speech sounds over and over again. They imitate the language they hear, which is reinforced by other adults, which helps them in developing more complex speech patterns. Children also acquire the ability to internalize speech and think about what they are saying.

Through a supportive relationship children learn to understand that speech is a language code. Where children are encouraged to talk about their experiences, their thinking is supported, but where children are not part of a language-rich environment, thinking and vocabulary may be limited. Children who are stressed, unwell, or under pressure may also find it difficult to express their thoughts and feelings.

Relationships and culture

The 'microsystem' of the family will have its own set of values and beliefs; in other words its own culture, which will have been influenced by a wider 'macrosystem' of values, for example, media and religion. These family values will shape the expectations and rules for behaviour and children will learn whether it is appropriate to act in certain ways. For example, in some families the expression of anger may not be allowed whilst in others children are allowed to express anger and are supported in dealing with it and developing appropriate modes of expression.

Through interaction with others, children learn the language and meaning of their culture. This enables them to express their ideas and cultural values. The language and values of pre-school may be vastly different from those of home. Children will need the support of good relationships in order to adjust and understand the language and values of this new context.

These initial relationships give children the message that they are cared and thought about. This lays the foundation for their mental well-being and their ability to think and learn.

Stimulation

In Chapter 2 you read about how the quality and effectiveness of thinking is dependent on how many connections and pathways are developed in the brain, especially between 0 and 7 years. Sensory, social and cultural stimulation is important in the development of the brain and complex thinking. Children have a natural curiosity to explore their world and a richer environment will help them develop more effectively. Children therefore need a wide range of first-hand experiences with real objects, which require exploration through the use of all their senses. Experiences such as sharing stories, rhymes and songs as well as social experiences will stimulate their language and communication development, as well as their thinking. Where this rich stimulating environment is enhanced by warm, caring, positive interactions, emotional well-being is supported and children come to associate learning with pleasure.

Health

We know that the health of the mother prior to and after birth can affect the development of the young infant. Poor diet, smoking, drug and alcohol abuse are all factors that may affect the long-term health and growth of the child.

Childhood nutrition and illnesses may also affect particular aspects of development. For example, children with temporary but frequent hearing-loss due to childhood ear problems may be delayed in their language development as well as suffering difficulty in interacting with peers and in forming friendships. Poor diet and nutrition may affect brain development at a time when a child's brain is undergoing important changes; this in turn will affect intellectual development.

The environment

Children are more likely to have positive self-concept when their physical and psychological needs are met. By this we mean food, water, warmth and sleep as well as stability, affection, rules, boundaries and positive relationships. These aspects will influence their development in all areas and lead to personal growth.

Poverty is one influence on the environment we know has a detrimental effect on the child. It affects basic provision that in some cases leads to a transient lifestyle and family stress, all of which impact on mental and physical health.

The environment and intellectual development

Children need to be able to engage socially and interact with their environment confidently in order to develop their language and communication skills, their capacity to think rationally and logically, their mathematics and science concepts and their ability to think creatively to find new ways of doing things, solve problems and make informed decisions.

The environment and physical development

From birth to seven years is a period of great change. Children develop large muscle control and big movements starting with the head, and later small muscles and finer movements.

Initially a reflex action, they then learn, practise and refine until movements become automatic. During this process children learn to mentally plan, organize and perform movements. They develop balance, speed, agility, power and coordination. They increase body, spatial and directional awareness by taking perceptual cues from the environment. Information is sent to the brain via the senses.

The space and opportunities available for children to explore their bodies and its capabilities will affect their physical development. Frequent opportunity to play outdoors will facilitate children's mastery over their own bodies as well as improve other areas of development and health. You will recall that Bruner emphasizes the importance of movement as a mode of learning. Children who do not have access to the rich experience of the outdoors will be slower to master and develop their bodies and the necessary cognitive structures for later, more complex thinking.

Gender

By about four years of age children have come to understand their sex is constant and they begin developing gender roles. Gender roles are learned through social reinforcement, that is, cultural influences or feedback from significant people in their lives. The role models that parents provide will have significant influence on the child's identification of gender role. Gender roles are also learned by imitating others of the same sex and through the expectations set by society of how they should behave according to their sex. We know from observations that gender affects the way in which children operate. Where children have experience of limited sex roles, for example, where mum always does the cooking and shopping and dad the DIY, they are restricted in their view of how men and women behave. Children therefore need the opportunity, and in some cases encouragement, to engage in a range of experiences that will extend their ideas of sex roles and provide the chance for them to negotiate sex roles in their play.

Figure 3.1 Children need opportunities in their play to extend their ideas of sex-roles

Play

The importance of play in development

Children have a natural instinct to learn about the world and much of this they do through play. Healthy, active and confident children are more likely to immerse themselves in a range of experiences, in order to acquire knowledge and understanding about all aspects of everyday life. We know from the work of Piaget and Vygotsky that children learn by being active rather than being passive observers. More meaningful learning takes place when they are able to construct it for themselves. Through social interactions with their peers and adults in their community they are supported in making sense of the world, they learn new concepts and become aware of their internal thoughts. Children are therefore active learners in a social context. Through play the whole child is actively engaged. Play supports them in making sense of their environment and culture and every aspect of their development; in other words, concepts and ideas, interactions, emotional well-being and physical development. Anything that influences children's ability or limits opportunities for play will affect their development.

How development affects learning and dispositions to learning

All aspects of children's development influence learning. We consider these aspects separately but you will see they are inter-related. Progression or regression in one area will impact on the others and we have already looked at some of the influences that may affect this rate of development.

Physical development and its influences on learning

Through movement children are developing intellectually. Through repetition of action, connections are made in the brain. The more complex the movement or pattern created, the greater the cognitive process. Children explore their environment, manipulate tools and learn new skills, with greater control and dexterity. Their ability to plan and organize their movements influences their ability to write, draw, and manipulate fine objects as well as develop their gross motor skills. For example, the development of fine motor control enables children to master writing tools. This gives them the opportunity to represent language in symbols for themselves. By repetition and practice children also master control over their bodies, thus developing physical competence and spatial awareness. This gives them confidence to interact with people and thus gain socially and linguistically. It enables them to join in with physical activity, be healthy, improve skills and be confident in tackling new things.

Figure 3.2 Through movement children are developing both physically and intellectually

Language development and influences on learning

Through language children express their ideas and feelings and describe their experiences. In Chapter 2 we talked of the role of language in the development of thinking. Children use language to control the world around them, reorganize meaning and represent their understanding. They do this by talking to themselves (egocentric talk). This private speech develops articulation and their ability to practise and plan different language structures. They are internalizing language, which develops thinking. It allows them to express their thoughts out loud, which helps them to connect and embed their ideas. Positive relationships encourage communication and are therefore an important factor in language development and thinking. From birth, babies recognize the sounds belonging to the language of their culture. Later they understand that sounds are words and begin to label objects. Through conversations children imitate language, listen and adapt their speech and use of language. They learn to interpret meaning. Language accompanied by action helps children to understand what is being said. Where relationships are poor and children have not experienced a rich language environment they have limited 'tools for thinking', limited language with which to represent their understanding and express their feelings.

Social and emotional development and its influences on learning

Sociable children can interact appropriately in order to learn from their peer group, parents and other adults. This means they have the necessary skills to cooperate in a group situation. They are able to take both a lead and subsidiary role in decision-making and stick to decisions made. They are aware of the needs of others and can understand different viewpoints and perspectives and how one event may affect another. They learn to develop socially acceptable behaviour in different circumstances. From a gender point of view they are making sense of the expectations, attitudes and behaviours set by the particular society or culture in which they function. They are influenced by stereotypical activities, feedback and role models.

Emotional intelligence is the ability to acknowledge feelings and emotions, understand their meaning and to use this information to focus thinking towards action and achieving a task.

> ...emotional intelligence is a master aptitude, a capacity that profoundly affects all other abilities, either facilitating or interfering with them (Goleman 1996: 80).

Goleman (1996) talks of five abilities associated with emotional intelligence: self-awareness, managing emotions, motivating oneself, recognizing emotions in others and handling relationships. He suggests that emotional health is fundamental to effective learning.

Where children are fearful and anxious, angry, have unrealistic expectations of themselves or lack confidence in their ability, they are unable to recognize and manage positive emotions, which hinders thought processes and memory and also their ability to channel their thinking into the learning task. Happy children, who can read and interpret their emotions and those of others, are more likely to be confident, motivated, display self-control, cooperate and be curious, all of which are essential dispositions to learning.

Emotionally able children tackle new situations confidently; they appreciate the value of friendship and show altruistic behaviour. They can pretend to be someone or something else. They are able to express their own feelings and emotions openly, which enables them to appreciate art, music and dance and be imaginative, innovative and creative. They can be resilient and cope with their anxieties. Emotional upheaval at sometime in children's lives may impact negatively upon learning, which in turn may affect their self-esteem. Their ability to manage their feelings and cope with stress can make a difference to whether they are successful learners or not.

Play and its influence on children's learning

We previously looked at the influence of children's development on the way in which they play. We will now consider how play influences children's learning and the necessary dispositions for lifelong learning. In other words their ability to make choices and direct their play, the level to which they are motivated to explore their environment and be adventurous, the confidence with which they can interact and cooperate with others and finally their ability to collaborate with and learn from their peers and adults affect learning throughout life.

The play environment will also influence children's learning: the extent to which it enables them to immerse themselves in something of interest for long periods of engagement, the variety of experiences offered, allowing children to make connections in their learning and the level to which children are supported in order to develop their learning. This is explored in more depth in Chapter 5.

Activity 3.3: Personal learning journal

Purpose:

- To understand the impact development may have on children's learning and how this influences the way in which children play
- To consider children's individual differences when planning play provision and intervention

In this activity you are going to carry out a time sample observation for one hour.

Every 15 minutes record the sex (M or F) and number of children in each area of provision and whether an adult was present. Table 3.1 is an example of how you might lay out your recording pro forma.

Table 3.1 An example of a time sample recording pro forma

Date of Observation_____
Number of adults in session____
Start time_____ End time_____

Write in the areas of provision in your setting.

Record the number of children at every 15-minute sample, across a 1-hour period.

Circle where an adult is present.

Areas/ activities	Sample 1 MF	Sample 2 MF	Sample 3 MF	Sample 4 MF
Sand	4 1			
Water	2 2			
Role play	1 3			

Use the following questions to help you reflect and make notes on what you have noticed:

- Do some activities seem more attractive to boys or girls, and if so which?
- Was there a relationship between the number of children and whether an adult was present?
- Were you surprised by anything from your observation?

Further activity

Identify how your observations relate to what you have read in the chapter.

Activity 3.4 Personal learning journal

In this activity you are going to carry out three narrative observations. (See Chapter 1 for details of this method.) From your observations in Activity 3.3 above, select (1) a female-dominated provision area, (2) a neutral-dominated provision area and (3) a male-dominated area.

Make an observation recording pro forma for each observation. Make sure you include basic contextual information as described in Chapter 1, Methods of observation.

Now observe what the children do and say whilst playing in each chosen provision area for a set period of time.

Use the following questions to help you reflect and make notes on what you have noticed:

- Does gender influence the way in which children play, and if so, in what way?
- What are the consequences for children's learning?

Activity 3.5: Further activity

In the activities above you have considered gender in isolation from other aspects of development. Make notes from your reading and your observations on the way in which gender may impact upon other aspects of development and influence learning.

Activity 3.6: Team meeting

Using your notes and observations, discuss the following questions:

- Does gender influence the provision area in which children choose to play, and if so, in what way?
- Does the presence of an adult influence the provision area in which children choose to play, and if so, how?
- Does gender influence the way in which children play in a chosen provision area, and if so, how?
- What are the implications for children's learning?

To conclude your team discussion, consider any changes you might make to your current practice as a result of your observations.

Further activity

As an individual consider and make notes on what you have learned and the level to which you were able to contribute to the team discussion. Identify areas you would like to know more about and follow this through with further observations and reading. Keep your notes for later in the chapter.

Activity 3.7: Further activity

- Choose a child whose play you think is highly influenced by one aspect of her development, e.g. emotional development such as low self-esteem, negative feelings, and anger. This may or may not be your target child depending on whether you feel they are influenced in a particular way.
- Choose an appropriate method of observation, e.g. event sampling or narrative observation. Remember to add contextual details when devising your pro forma.
- Observe the child during the course of a week in their play activities/experiences, focusing on your chosen aspect of development.
- Analyse your observations by identifying the ways in which the aspect of development influences their play, and any emerging patterns.
- What have you learned about the child? Now write a brief summary for use in the team meeting.

Further activity

In drawing conclusions from your observations refer also to the learning theories in Chapter 2 as well as your reading of this chapter. Now write a brief summary for use in the team meeting.

Team meeting

All team members should explain why they chose their particular child to observe and the observations they made before presenting their summaries.

From the three activities above you have begun to build up pictures of the children's development and learning in your setting. You should be noticing differences in the children and the way in which they have different needs and be able to relate this to learning and developmental theory. The children in your setting will probably constitute a breadth of stages of development.

- From the play experiences your setting provides, give examples that might support the aspect of development you observed
- To conclude your team discussion, consider any changes you might make to your current practice in terms of the experiences you provide

Further activity

As an individual be conscious when you are making your contributions to this meeting of the level to which you are able to justify your conclusions by referring to the theories and your additional reading so far.

Activity 3.8: Personal learning journal

This activity involves completing a personal learning journal record sheet (see Table 0.2 in the Introduction). Use your notes from Activity 3.7 above. In the first section of the record sheet, briefly describe what you did for each of the team meetings. In the next section reflect on your contribution to these meetings: your ability to interpret information from your observations and explain this to the team, your ability to listen to others and draw on their experiences to develop your own skills and your understanding of what is involved in meeting children's individual needs. Identify information you need to gather in order to help you with this analysis. Refine your thinking and identify your strengths and weaknesses as a team member. Now, in the third section, say what action you will take in order to improve your contributions to future team meetings. You might make a checklist to use for monitoring. In the final section evaluate how well you have improved your understanding and skills as a team member.

Return to your ideas map from Activity 3.2. Add to it any other influences you have thought about and identify any connections. Keep your ideas map and return to it when you read Chapter 10 on Planning.

Summary

This chapter should have raised your awareness of some of the social and cultural influences on children's development, the holistic nature of development and how this affects learning. You have begun to consider the importance of the play provision and experiences in meeting individual needs. We will summarize by further considering implications for practice.

Aspects of development are interrelated and all influence the child's ability to learn. Intellectual development is closely connected with social and cooperative skills, and emotional intelligence can either foster or hinder a child's ability to access learning and achieve their goals. Where basic needs are not met and children are physically unwell then learning is also limited.

The pre-school setting is only one in a range of cultural and social contexts that will influence developing children. Their ability to manage differing rules and expectations of each context will affect their development and learning. Recognizing and celebrating the culture and language of home will enable children to feel valued and included.

The inter-relationship between contexts should be such that the child is supported. The setting's ability, therefore, to understand and work with parents and family, relevant health and social services, and other providers such as childminders, will be a supportive influence on development and learning.

Developing strong, positive relationships with individual children supports them in all aspects of their development and gives them confidence to engage with the environment and benefit from learning experiences. Children learn from people they like and who give them positive feedback. This is particularly crucial when children are not well supported in other contexts.

Children's development influences the way in which they play. Anything which affects children's natural curiosity to explore and make discoveries will obviously restrict their learning. However, children also need access to a rich, stimulating environment and a range of interesting experiences in which to play in order to facilitate their curiosity and support them in developing an understanding of the world and the necessary dispositions for lifelong learning.

Jargon explained

Altruistic behaviour: this is where children are intrinsically motivated to help and care for others. They do not expect any concrete reward for this and recognize there may be some detriment to or sacrifice for themselves.

Self-image: this means a sense of identity, the mental image the child builds of herself as a result of interpreting her perceptions of how others view her.

Self-concept: is the inner picture the child has of herself, her capability, self-worth and attractiveness. In other words, a combination of self-image and self-esteem.

Self-esteem: is established by the child comparing her self-image with an 'ideal self'.

Gender: the roles assigned to each sex by the culture in which they live.

Further reading

Selleck, D. (2004), 'Being under 3 years of age: enhancing quality experiences', in Miller, L. and Devereux, J. (eds) (2004), *Supporting Children's Learning in the Early Years*. London: David Fulton.

This chapter looks at how the role of the practitioner in early years settings might support and enhance the learning, play and care of under-threes in their families. It discusses attachment, the importance of the key worker, observation and the need to provide a curriculum that meets the diverse interests and ways in which children under three learn.

Siraj-Blatchford, I. and Clarke, P. (2004), 'Identity, self-esteem and learning', in Miller, L. and Devereux, J. (eds) (2004), *Supporting Children's Learning in the Early Years*. London: David Fulton.

This chapter explores the factors that can lead to children being disadvantaged and identifies the features of effective practice in promoting respect for all of those involved in early years settings.

It looks at identity and its connection with achievement, diversity and equality and self-esteem. It presents a set of stages for discussion around discriminatory practice.

References

Bronfenbrenner, U. (1979), 'The ecology of human development', in Smith, P.K., Cowie, H. and Blades, M. (2003), *Understanding Children's Development*. 4th edn. Oxford: Blackwell.

Goleman, G. (1996), *Emotional Intelligence: Why it Can Matter More than IQ*. London: Bloomsbury.

4 Key Ideas that Inform us about Learning Through Play

Chapter Outline

Introduction   70
Young children are competent and experienced learners   72
Children's learning is influenced by significant others   73
Language is a central mechanism in learning   75
Learning can be scaffolded   78
Observation can help us understand and support children's thinking   79
Learning and development in one area can affect learning in all others   79
Children learn best when actively involved in learning   81
Jargon explained, References   82

Introduction

This chapter takes a thematic approach, drawing together information from the previous two chapters about the key ideas that underpin our understanding of effective learning through play in pre-school.

Purpose of this chapter

The seven key themes that are to be outlined will form a coherent structure in which to think about effective pre-school education; they draw together all you have learned about young children as learners in a way that can help you reflect on how this knowledge might affect your practice.

Activity 4.1: Team meeting

Before you begin the chapter, complete the following activity in small groups.

Purpose: To heighten your awareness of how we make sense of things and how we learn most effectively.

Resources:

- The word 'apple' on a sheet of paper
- A line drawing of an apple
- A photograph of an apple
- An apple
- A knife
- A magnifying glass

Instead of an apple, another fruit or vegetable that can be eaten raw can be used. Ideally it would be a fruit or vegetable with which the group were unfamiliar, although such an object might be a little difficult to find.

Preparation

Groups may have up to five members. Where there are more than five people in the team, you will need to work in two or more groups, each group having access to the full range of resources.

Activity

- As a group try to learn as much as you can about the object you have, exploring each source of information using all your senses. Draw only on information you gain from the resources themselves and not from any prior knowledge you have, for example, your knowledge of what the word means. During the activity it might help to try to imagine you have never come across an apple before and that the word is in a foreign language you do not speak.
- The group should first work with the word on the sheet. Note everything the word 'apple' can tell you about the object it represents.
- The group then moves on to the drawing and then the photograph going through the same procedure. Question closely any information you think the item gives you.
- Finally work with the apple.

Feedback

Now consider the following questions (where there is more than one group, share this part of the activity):

Activity 4.1 (continued)

- Which 'object' gave you most information?
- How did you find the information about the object?
- Did you discover anything that you did not know?
- What supported this learning?

Consider these points after you have completed the activity:

- What should emerge from this activity is the fact that words are meaningless unless they represent an experience you have had of something.
- Line drawings give very limited information other than the outline shape; they are still, like words, symbolic rather than iconic. Even the photograph adds only colour and a sense of the object's three-dimensional nature. The only sense you can use in exploring these resources is sight.
- The apple itself allowed you to gather much more information; perhaps things you had not noticed before. Key to this was active learning and multi-sensory experience. You were able to handle the fruit, feel its weight, smell it, taste it, look closely at it and perhaps listen to the rattle of the seeds before you cut into it. You worked at your own pace, doing the things that helped you explore, you will have talked together, shared ideas and expressed ideas in words.

It is only when we have experienced the world, and can draw on this experience, that secondary sources such as drawings, photographs and words can make sense to us. Consider how often we use secondary sources with children before they have had the experience to make sense of them.

Young children are competent and experienced learners

Underpinning all effective practice is the image the practitioner has of the child as a competent learner. All that research has uncovered about young children reinforces the view that from birth they are competent and effective learners predisposed to make sense of the world, to actively seek experiences that assist them in making sense of the world. Piaget's early interest in learning emerged from observing his own young babies playing in their cots, exploring the objects around them.

Most children by the time they are one year old have begun to use verbal sound to communicate; by two years they are talking in short sentences and by three years they have mastered pronouns such as I, you, me, we, and they. However, although children do this most effectively within the context of a family life where they have rich and varied experiences, they actually develop language independently with the minimum of planned adult intervention, in the form of interaction about everyday life or play with adults as play partners.

From the beginnings of their lives children develop different ways of learning through their play; they use their senses in an increasingly sophisticated way; their brain structure expands and they build up a secure understanding of how their world works.

> **Key message for settings**: Practitioners need to understand the child in terms of what they can do and not what they cannot do.

Children's learning is influenced by significant others

The importance of the child's relationships with others cannot be over emphasized. They form the bedrock of children's lives and influence their development in all its aspects. 'Others' are the looking glass through which the child comes to know herself; they are the source of her tools for thinking and communicating; they provide the model for her social, moral and emotional development. Positive and supportive relationships in early life form a strong foundation for later life.

The relationships the child forms in the early years setting are crucial to her learning; the experience the child has with early years teachers is important in the process of lifelong learning. We know that learning dispositions are established in early childhood and it is these attitudes that can shape the learner's experience of learning and approach to learning throughout their lives. We also know from our understanding of the spiral curriculum and from recent brain studies that skills, concepts and knowledge gained during early childhood are utilized for more complex learning in later life. As far back as the sixteenth century the Jesuits' saying 'Give me a child until he is seven and I will give you the man' reflected their experience that early education and experience had lifelong consequences.

> **Key message for settings**: Early years practitioners must be aware of the significance of their relationship with every child. This relationship will help the child begin a journey that will last a lifetime and, as with all journeys, the enthusiasm with which they begin and the direction in which they set off will greatly influence how they will fare on that journey.

Familial, peer and wider cultural gender expectations encourage us to take stereotypical gender roles, to behave in gender-specific ways. These restrictions limit our experience of the world and how we act upon it and therefore they restrict our learning.

> **Key message for settings**: Practitioners need to monitor their own interaction with children to ensure they do not reinforce stereotypic behaviour and to ensure that boys and girls experience all the setting has to offer.

Children's physical and mental health is influenced directly by the health of their mother, during pregnancy, and later by the quality of the care she or other carers provide. In turn their mental and physical health may affect their development, their play and their opportunities to interact with peers.

> **Key message for settings**: Practitioners need to take into account any health problems children might have, or have had, when planning to meet individual needs. Of course where children do not receive the appropriate quality of care at home and are coming to harm, the setting has a statutory duty to alert the appropriate body.

The quality of the environment is an important influence on the child. In order to flourish, children need to feel safe, secure and valued; they need to be provided with a healthy diet and a lifestyle that ensures sufficient sleep, fresh air, exercise and healthy surroundings. The physical environment of the child both at home and in the early years setting influences her in several ways. First, in terms of physical development, which is influenced by the space the child has to move in; second, in terms of health and opportunities for exercise and fresh air; and finally, in terms of stimulation and the opportunities for play the environment offers. The child's experiences as a player will influence how, and how well, she plays. The emotional and social environment in which a child grows influences positively or negatively her emotional and social development; these in turn influence her dispositions and relationships with others.

> **Key message for settings**: Practitioners need to be aware of the importance of the physical and emotional environment they provide.

Language is a central mechanism in learning

We learn in different ways and our memories are stored in different forms; as actions, as images and as symbols and language. The most powerful of these forms is language, which allows us to think in more complex ways, to understand the thoughts of others and to share our thoughts with them. In sharing words and language structures with children we share our vision and understanding of the world, we initiate them into our culture and our ways of seeing things.

> **Key message for settings**: Children need rich and varied language in order to think about and to learn about the world around them. They need adults who will support their thinking by introducing them to the language they need as they explore and play.
>
> The role of children's own talk and other forms of representation is important in learning.

Children need to talk; take talk away from them and you impoverish their learning. Young children are learning quickly, learning new things every day, adding to their understanding, building their internal 'pictures' of the world and how it works. This process involves the development of thinking. Although for adults thinking is usually internal dialogue, for very young children it is still largely in the form of 'speech for themselves'; this form of speech is still a feature of their learning and thinking. Children talk their thoughts; this helps them to build up their mental structures.

Children also need to share their thoughts and feelings with others, to try out ideas, to come to some judgement about their validity, to negotiate meaning in dialogue with others, especially more knowledgeable others.

Talk is also one of the main mechanisms through which children learn to cooperate with others, to understand how to negotiate and come to shared ways of doing things.

We now understand that other forms of representation are also very important for children's developing brains. Play allows the development of a range of representational modes such as drawing, dance, music and modelling.

Figure 4.1 In play children can talk for a range of purposes

Key message for settings: Settings need to provide space, time, materials and encouragement so that children are able to represent their learning and understanding in different ways. In play children have control over their actions and their representations; they can use talk for a range of purposes, they can try out new ways of representing things, they can express ideas, negotiate play scripts all without fear of getting it wrong.

Activity 4.2: Personal learning journal

Purpose: To raise awareness of the range of representational modes your children use.

Observe your children playing using a simple narrative record. Look for examples of the children's use of talk: gather two examples of egocentric talk, peer talk, adult/child talk (and baby utterances if you are with very young children). Note especially what they say, how long their utterances are and how many turns there are in the conversation.

Look for examples of other ways in which children have represented ideas.

Further activity

Analyse your observations in terms of:

- the range of talk functions and where they occurred
- the range of other forms of representation and where they occurred
- how the type of talk the child uses varies according to its purpose

Activity 4.3: Team meeting

Share the following information:

- Which activities generate most talk?
- Which activities generate other forms of representation?
- What does the information you have shared tell you about the range of modes of representation the play in your setting supports?
- Do some activities support more representation than others?

(Keep the observational material for further analysis in Activity 4.4.)

Further activity

Highlight the types of activities that generate the greatest range of forms of representation. For example, on the painting table children may use talk, movement and graphic forms to express and explore ideas. Does the group notice a pattern in relation to the types of talk different play activities generate?

Learning can be scaffolded

Children build their own learning. This process does not, however, occur in isolation; it occurs within the context of the child's community and is supported by the child's interactions with others and with materials within that community. These interactions and materials provide a supporting framework for the child's learning; they facilitate the development of her ideas much as scaffolding supports the house builder.

Successful support for children's thinking takes account of what the individual child is learning. This support may be linguistic or non-verbal communication, or the provision of additional objects or materials. Successful scaffolding is that which supports thinking without diverting it from the direction that interests, and serves the needs of, the child. It is also that which when removed does not result in the collapse of the learning process.

Key message for settings: Practitioners need to think about and provide support for children's thinking that takes account of what the individual child is concerned with learning. What the adult does has a strong influence on the child and so scaffolding needs to be sensitive, responsive and timely; it needs to draw on a range of strategies.

Activity 4.4: Personal learning journal

Purpose: To highlight the influence of the adult on children's representation of their understanding.

Return to your previous observation notes and analyse the talk in terms of the number of words, balance of talk between those involved and whether the talk was about the activity.

Compare the child's communication when alone, with peers and with an adult.

Further activity

- Consider the effectiveness of verbal communication as a vehicle for expressing the child's thinking
- Compare the quality of the child's communication in terms of length, turn taking and content when alone, with peers and with an adult

Activity 4.5: Team meeting

During a team meeting the staff should consider the following key questions:

- Were there any differences in the communication between the following categories: boys and girls; younger and older children; peer discussion compared with adult/child communication?
- Did adult intervention help the child's thinking?

Further activity

Additionally, consider how adults influenced the nature of interaction.

Observation can help us understand and support children's thinking

In play children will be performing at the upper boundary of what they can achieve alone; careful observation of children at play will allow practitioners to decide the child's level of independent activity and determine their current fascinations and concerns (sometimes through action schema). Understanding and recognizing the ideas that young children are currently grappling with, in their attempts to build up their understanding of the world, is one way of finding out what we as adults can do to support their learning.

Key message for settings: Knowledge gathered through the observation of children playing supports practitioners in providing appropriate and well-focused scaffolding for the child's learning.

Learning and development in one area can affect learning in all others

In the early years of education there has been a long tradition of addressing the needs of the 'whole child'. Pre-schools have been concerned with physical, social and emotional well-being alongside concerns about the child's intellectual and linguistic development. What is now clear is the significant impact that each area of development has on the others. The implications for practitioners are huge; in planning for children's play they need to consider not only the balance of experiences but also the needs of the individual child across all areas of their development; play must offer children a multitude of ways of exploring, learning and expression.

Effective early years play provision requires consideration of aspects of the child's individual make-up, for example, the enormous impact that self-concept has on all-round development is now well documented. This demands that the adults who work with young children reflect on their practice and provision in terms of how well it supports the development of positive self-concept. The EPPE (Sylva et al. 2004) research found that settings that view cognitive and social development as complementary achieve the best outcomes.

> **Key message for settings**: Practitioners need to provide play opportunities that draw on and support a range of developmental areas.

Figure 4.2 Practitioners need to provide play opportunities that support all areas of development. Think about which area this activity supports

Activity 4.6: Personal learning journal

Purpose: To reflect on the influence of early experiences.

- Start by thinking about the influence of your own early experiences and the influence they have had on your life
- Now think about one particular child you have worked with. Reflect on the changes in the child's play and development over the time with you; think about the opportunities you gave the child to develop all of his or her skills and talents. You may wish to share this with your team although this is not necessary

Further activity

Try to identify the influences on the child's learning in terms of the issues highlighted in this chapter.

Children learn best when actively involved in learning

The next key idea is that of the child being an active rather than a passive learner. There is now overwhelming evidence that we all learn best if we can be active in the learning process; for young children this is even more essential to their learning. Think back to the apple activity and the difference between learning from secondary sources and learning by working with the real object. Language, resources, time and first-hand experience with real materials supported this learning.

Contexts that support active learning give the child the opportunity to:

- have first-hand experience of the things about which they are learning
- be active in the construction of their own knowledge of the world through experiences that have meaning for them
- represent their thoughts and ideas using a range of expressive forms
- interact with adults who are knowledgeable, observant and sensitive, who are able to work alongside them, share their learning and support their thinking and representation
- spend the time they need to develop their ideas, to become deeply involved and immersed in activities
- make thoughtful choices and decisions about what resources they use and how they use them
- pursue their current concerns (schema, interests), as these represent those areas of learning the child is constructing
- initiate activity in which they can use all their senses and explore in different ways

Key message for settings: Self-initiated play supported by adults is the most powerful opportunity for active learning.

Jargon explained

Non-verbal communication: consists of a range of features used to aid expression often used subconsciously. The main components are: body language such as shrugs; eye movements such as winking; facial expressions; gestures; touch; eye contact; quality of voice such as tone, volume, speed or other sounds; posture.

Talk functions: the range of purposes for which talk is used, for example, informing, questioning, greeting, and expressing feelings.

References

Sylva, K., Melhuish, E., Sammons, P., Siraj-Blatchford, I. and Taggart, B. (2004), *Effective Provision of Pre-School Education Project*. DfES.

Part Two
PLAY AND ITS ROLE IN PRE-SCHOOL EDUCATION

Play and Learning 5

Chapter Outline

Introduction	85
What do we mean by play?	86
Play in the educational context	87
How does good quality play support learning?	91
What do we mean by good quality play?	95
Key aspects of play	96
Types of play and their importance	98
Summary, Further reading, References	103

Introduction

Since far back in history great thinkers have recognized the importance of play. In the sixth century BC Heraclitus of Ephesus claimed that, 'Man is most nearly himself when he achieves the seriousness of a child at play'. In the fifth century BC Plato recognized play as a powerful vehicle for learning:

> Because for a free man learning should never be associated with slavery. Physical exertion, imposed by force, does the body no harm, but for the soul no forced learning can be lasting [...] when you're bringing up children don't use compulsion in teaching them. Use children's games instead. (Plato 2000: 246)

More recently Piaget and Vygotsky have extolled the virtues of play in the learning process. Play features in most adults' lives to a greater or lesser extent, but for all children play is a prominent and essential part of their lives; it is a necessary element in their developmental processes. Play is of central importance to the child's intellectual, social, emotional, physical and linguistic development; it is therefore a necessity not a luxury for them. Play is a feature of all societies. As Jensen and Scott (1980: 296) claim, 'Play...is a cross-cultural universal, expressing in an almost unlimited variety of ways the primal biological urge to move, explore, discover, risk, text, master, create and – of paramount importance – have fun.' So strong is the belief across the world that children have the right to play that it is enshrined in the United Nations Declaration of the Rights of the Child:

> The child shall have full opportunity for play and recreation, which should be directed to the same purposes as education; society and the public authorities shall endeavour to promote the enjoyment of this right
> (Principle 7, United Nations resolution 1386 (XIV) of 20 November 1959).

Purpose of this chapter

To help you think about how play supports children's learning. It will support you in explaining to parents and other interested parties why you use play. In particular we will look at how play relates to what we have learned in the previous chapters.

What do we mean by play?

The arguments about what counts as play are numerous and complex. Although most people will happily label activities as play and non-play and there have been many attempts to provide a definitive description of play (see, for example, Bennett et al. 1997, Moyles 1994, and Bruce 1991), there remains no unanimous agreement on a definition of play. In everyday life we refer to many different activities as play: playing with bricks, playing in the water, playing with a train set, playing football, playing poker and playing hard to get! We will not debate here what counts as play but simply explain what we mean by play in the educational context using terms familiar to the practitioner and quotes from key writers.

Activity 5.1: Personal learning journal

Purpose: To begin to use your knowledge of children's learning to inform your understanding of play.

Return to your notes and ideas map from the initial activities about play in the Introduction. Now you have read about children's learning and the influences on it, have any of your ideas changed? Can you identify that what you seem to value most about play is related to how children learn? Add your new ideas to your original ideas map or chart using another colour.

Play in the educational context

Play is a generic term that is applied to a wide range of activities and behaviours. In all contexts, play is a form of activity that exhibits particular characteristics related to the player's creativity, control, engagement, enjoyment, motivation and purpose and in which the viewpoint and perception of the player are predominant.

Jerome Bruner suggested that the main characteristic of play was not its content but its form. He said that play was about how action was approached and not what kind of activity it was. This seems a good starting point; it defines play in terms of the child's disposition and action behaviours rather than what activity he is involved in. This allows us to identify play as an approach to action that exists in a continuum of the various types of 'play' characterized by the roles of the child and the parallel role of the adult. The continuum moves from free-flow play (Bruce 1991) where the child's activity is self-initiated, and follows entirely their agenda, to activities that might best be described as playful teaching such as the use of number games in a mathematics lesson, which are teacher initiated and follow the teacher's agenda (see Table 5.1).

Table 5.1 The play continuum

Free-flow play	Structured play	Guided play	Playful teaching
Child control			Adult control

The following are the definitions of the kinds of play we have noted above.

Free-flow play

The activity is self-initiated, freely chosen, free from any external imperatives, is intrinsically worthwhile, is flexible following entirely the player's agenda, a process that is open ended, with no predetermined outcome, involves active engagement and is enjoyable for the individual. The adult sets the resources up with, perhaps, generic learning opportunities in mind; she may or may not become involved; if she does she will take her lead from the child.

Example: a table is set up in the room with a quantity of clay and a bowl of water with various clay tools in a box in the middle. Children decide to play with the clay; they explore its texture, build it into tall piles and make holes in it. One child flattens his piece of clay and uses the tools to make patterns on the flattened disc; another goes to get twigs and stones from the found materials box and sticks them into the clay. The children talk about what they are doing sometimes to themselves and sometimes to the other child. The adult observes but decides not to intervene as she judges that the play is developing well without her support.

Structured play

The activity is self-managed and the child is free to use the materials as he decides but he may have been directed to the play; the resources are planned by the adult with specific intended learning outcomes in mind based on assessment of the learning needs of the children. The adult may or may not become involved but if she does although she will take account of what the child is concerned with, she will also have the intended learning outcomes in mind.

Example: the setting is following a theme that is centred on a visit to a garden centre. The practitioner wants children to have experience of counting (ELG MD – early learning goals, mathematical development), using language to create roles (ELG CLL – early learning goals, communication language and literacy) and working as part of a group (ELG PSED – early learning goals, personal social emotional development) but with particular focus on the ELGs of knowledge and understanding of the world. She sets up a garden centre in the room with these learning outcomes in mind; resources are chosen with particular play activities in mind. Children choose to go into this area during the session but she monitors this and towards the end of the week asks children who have not spent time in the area to work in there that day. On a regular basis she joins in the play providing the key vocabulary she has identified, highlighting areas of the experience that support her planned outcomes.

Figure 5.1 Structured play does not have to be complex and may be used to reinforce playful teaching

The following two modes, which form the right-hand end of the continuum, are commonly found in early years settings and do have elements of play in them. However, it is the first two modes of play that we have identified as having the characteristics of true play and with which this book is principally concerned.

Guided play

The activity is chosen by the adults with very specific activity and learning outcomes in mind; the child is given a goal. Children are asked to play in a specific way and often the material can only be used in limited ways. Children may be directed to the area on a rota. The activity is more directly managed by the adult who will often work with or alongside the children modelling and guiding their actions.

Example: the adult provides several simple jigsaws with the intention of developing the children's number concepts; she works alongside the children showing them what to do, joining in the puzzle, giving them instructions, reinforcing number recognition and counting. She provides a similar puzzle and encourages the children to complete them independently.

Playful teaching

The activity is chosen and rules laid down by the adult; the children may self-manage the play within these rules.

Example: the practitioner gathers her group of five children around a table; she has devised a simple counting game with one learning outcome (Foundation Stage Guidance, Mathematical Development, recognizes numbers one to nine). She explains the rules and supports each child as they throw the dice and cover that number on their game board. After two rounds she sits back and intervenes to support counting and when the children are in difficulties. The use of 'feely bags' (where objects are presented to children in bags and they have to guess what they are) in phonics teaching is another example of playful teaching.

Activity 5.2: Personal learning journal

Purpose: To clarify what each of the above categories of play is by identifying them in your setting.

- Stop at this point and identify activities within your setting that would equate to each of the categories on the continuum
- Observe one activity of each type. We suggest you observe intensively for about five minutes
- Note down what you notice about the roles of the adults and the roles of the children
- Make notes to support your feedback during the team meeting

Further activity

Which types of play do children engage in most, in which type do children get most adult attention, and which activities do adults spend most time planning and supporting?

Note your thoughts in your journal and we will return to them later.

Activity 5.3: Team meeting

Work to come to a consensus about where the activities you have observed come on the play continuum (see Table 5.1).

Further activity

Consider the following questions:

- In what kind of play do adults spend most of their time?
- Which kinds of play seem to have most status?
- Does the setting consciously value one approach more than another?

Play provides a context where the freedom from the pressure to produce or perform allows the child to be more intellectually adventurous; it develops learning processes and skills in such a way that children work beyond their normal level of operation.

The essence of play is the dominance of means over ends...in play the process is more important than the product. Freed from the tyranny of a tightly held goal, the player can substitute, elaborate and invent (Bruner et al. 1976: 244).

In play cognitive processes and learning skills are developed either consciously or instinctively, and contribute to the child's effectiveness as a learner. An essential characteristic of all play is its stress-free nature which allows children to explore ideas in a psychologically safe context. Jensen and Scott suggest that, 'Play is a miniature laboratory in which children are protected and allowed to experiment' (Jensen and Scott 1980: 296).

Play encourages high levels of motivation, concentration and sustained activity because it is self-chosen action and at the child's own pace. It supports the development of learning dispositions such as concentration and perseverance. In play, argued Vygotsky, children work at a higher level of cognitive functioning than they do in everyday life; they think in more complex ways and represent their thinking symbolically.

> ...play also creates the zone of proximal development for the child. In play a child is always above his average age, above his daily behaviour: in play it is as though he were a head taller than himself. As in the focus of a magnifying glass, play contains all the developmental tendencies in a condensed form; in play it is as though the child were trying to jump above the average level of his normal behaviour (Vygotsky 1978: 102).

Return to Chapter 2 if you are unsure what ZPD is. In play a child can achieve a higher, more conscious level of functioning; the experience enables the child to internalize the skill or knowledge and integrate it with his existing cognitive frameworks gaining independent and conscious control over it.

How does good quality play support learning?

Play allows children to learn actively; it engages the whole child

Play is an active form of learning that involves the whole self; it engages both brain and body; it draws on all the senses. Children in this television and computer generation often engage with the world through their sense of sight and hearing, but taste, touch, smell and the sense of motion that play may draw on are also powerful modes of learning. Play allows children opportunities to be immersed in complex experiences, to become aware of how they are thinking and feeling, to be alert and attentive not because there is pressure to achieve but because the activity makes sense to them and totally involves them. Play engages the child physically, intellectually, linguistically, socially and emotionally.

Play supports children in the development of concepts and ideas

The cross-curricular nature of play allows children to make connections and to build on concepts in different cognate areas simultaneously. Through the use of action schema (Athey; see Chapter 2) in play children systematically construct their understanding of the world by acting upon it in different ways. Play supports the spiral curriculum of learning, allowing children to revisit concepts and ideas in different ways and at different levels. Piaget felt that while children were still in the concrete stages, and unable to think abstractly, the direct experience of people and things that play offered allowed them to develop and refine concepts.

In contrasting adult play with that of children, Erikson (1984) highlights the important function of such play in helping the child to deal with real experiences by creating parallel play situations. He says that while for adults play is a step 'sideward into another reality', for children it advances mastery of reality as they create 'model' situations that allow them to try out and experiment with reality.

Play allows the child to begin separating thought from actions and objects. From birth using concrete objects and actions, exploratory play allows the child to build an internal model of the object or the action and to learn about its characteristics. Piaget called this mastery play and equated it to the sensory motor stage. Pretend play which occurs from about 18 months to two years signals a growing understanding of knowledge and belief, that is, knowing what is real and what is not. In pretend play where the child makes one object stand for another or one action stand for another, she takes her understanding of the world further towards symbolic thinking, towards mastering the meaning of the object or action. The play object or action is chosen to stand for (replace) the real thing because it can be used in a similar way to the actual object or action. For example, a spectacle case may stand for a telephone receiver while a ball could not. So through her play the child begins to separate the idea of the object or action from the thing itself through the use of an intermediate or pivot between the real and the imagined. This allows for the development of symbolic thought, that is, being able to think about an object or action in its absence. Piaget called this play, which occured during the pre-operational period, symbolic or make-believe play.

Play supports children's learning about their environment and their culture

Across all cultures play is a characteristic element of young children's lives. It is the way they explore and learn about the world around them. Children play with their culture's artefacts, learning what they do and about their significance. They explore the modes of expression in the culture; they play with language, draw, sing and move. In play children develop and practise the skills they need to operate successfully within their own environment; they gain the knowledge and understanding of how things are. Play allows them to make sense of adult roles within their society by re-enacting them in a pretend situation.

Figure 5.2 Play supports children's understanding of cultural representation such as music and number

Play supports children's social interaction and social development

Vygotsky recognized that play was a vehicle for social interaction, essential for learning, and an opportunity for children to develop confidence and mastery. In play children can try out ways of interacting, taking on different roles and persona. Although it is not done formally, during play children negotiate the rules of the play (Vygotsky 1966). In this way their social interaction is supported by the shared purposes of play and the agreed ways of doing things.

As complex collaborative play develops in the later years of early childhood, children practise and develop high-level skills of negotiation, empathy, cooperating, helping and sharing.

Play supports children's emotional development

You will recall from your reading of Chapter 3 that emotional development is about recognizing, understanding and controlling your own emotional responses within accepted cultural norms, being able to recognize the emotional response of others and being able to use this information to decide how to act appropriately. Play, especially role play, allows children to 'try on' emotional responses in a 'not serious' way and to learn about the responses of others. 'I'm only pretending', they can say. In play children can express and come to an understanding of the emotional aspects of their experiences. Play helps children to deal with their feelings and fears; to explore and manage their emotional states. Froebal (1887) argued that play is the highest level of child development, that it is an expression of thought and feeling that is a requirement of the child's 'inner life'. So powerful is play in supporting emotional development that it has led to the development of play therapy for children who are experiencing problems in this area of development.

Play helps children develop self-regulation

Play can also serve as a tool of the mind that enables children to master their own behaviour. Play provides some of the first constraints that cause children to channel, direct and organize their behaviours in specific ways. Play allows for imaginary situations that contain a set of rules and roles, allowing for the practising of regulating behaviours. In every play situation, even where the child is playing alone, ways of playing are developed; stated or unstated rules emerge from the play activity, which then require the child to direct her behaviour and to think about what she is doing. These rules are generated by the child and often mirror their perception of reality. For example, when playing 'families' they take on clearly understood roles which then determine their action.

Play enables children to integrate all that they know in order to understand new learning

Children's play is built on the knowledge and skills they have; they begin with the known and explore further. Play acts as a device that enables children to draw on experiences in their past, to represent their experience in different ways, to begin to make connections between the things they know and have experienced and the new experience, to see patterns and investigate. It allows them to try combinations of behaviours without the pressure to achieve a given goal. Piaget (1976) recognized that during their play children could combine existing knowledge, skills and understanding and apply them to new situations; in other words they could be problem solvers. Play helps children to make connections with ideas that they have already internalized. By integrating all of these elements, play allows the child to create a sense of meaning; it encourages new ways of seeing things.

Play provides an excellent opportunity for adults to scaffold learning

Scaffolding of learning during play can be particularly successful because, as children's own purposes and needs direct the play, they are more discernible to the observer and, as the child is working at his highest level, the adult can more easily gauge whether the level of challenge is within the child's ZPD. In play children understand what is happening, and control of the context allows them to be more confident partners in the negotiation and co-construction of knowledge. Play offers the opportunity for adults to help children see causal relationships, use different modes of expression and its flexibility allows them to use a range of scaffolding techniques. (See Chapter 9 for further discussion of this.)

What do we mean by good quality play?

All provision for play that fulfils the purposes we have discussed above has several features in common; it allows children to:

- physically manipulate the things in their environment
- learn through all their senses
- have the opportunity to engage in active learning
- learn within a meaningful social and cultural context
- work at their own pace
- make choices and decisions that matter to them
- be immersed in their own concerns (schema)
- be totally involved
- behave spontaneously
- explore ideas, feelings and emotions safely
- pretend, imagine and create
- be supported by adults who know how and when to support them

Good quality play allows for effective learning when it involves:

- creative and imaginative play activities that promote thinking and its expression through different modes of representation
- children making links in their learning that lead to more complex brain development
- children learning in different ways and at different rates

- children feeling secure and becoming confident learners
- children having time to explore ideas and interests in depth
- children initiating activity that promotes learning and enables them to learn from each other
- children taking control of their own learning
- the use of all the senses
- the opportunity to explore a rich range of natural and cultural artefacts
- encouragement and supportive interaction between children, their peers and the adults in the setting

So what would we expect the children to be doing where there is good quality play?

We should see sustained thinking, concentration, collaboration, pretence, imagination, creativity, role play, applying, practising, rehearsal, repetition, manipulating objects, tools and materials confidently, involvement, commitment, interest, perseverance and a secure emotional state.

Key aspects of play

Although no one aspect of play is discrete, and there are connections between them, we have chosen to highlight several particularly important individual aspects.

The social context of play: playing together

You will notice in your observations that the social context of play varies, again along a continuum; the more developmentally mature and experienced in play the child is the more likely they are to play in cooperative groups. Each form of play offers children different forms of engagement and learning opportunities.

Onlooker – the child actively observes others play perhaps learning through imitation or taking time to think about what they want to do. This might be on a regular basis or for an extended period of time. Although this behaviour is more common with younger children even adults involve themselves in this kind of activity.

Solitary – the child works alone with no reference to others, working through their own ideas and concerns, consolidating their understanding. When in solitary play the child may think about feelings, people and relationships, develop ideas in a deep and intense way which often unlocks creativity. This enables children to learn about themselves and, if feeling safe and secure, push themselves in their thinking.

Parallel – children play near each other with the same materials, are aware of each other but do not interact, working through their own ideas and concerns, consolidating their understanding but perhaps taking cues/ideas from those working around them. In parallel play children learn alongside each other by watching and understanding that they can influence someone else or be influenced themselves.

Group (associative) – children interact together during the activity often needing to coordinate activities and so take on the feelings and concerns of others. In associative play children can develop theories of mind (see Chapter 2), develop their collaborative skills and empathy.

Group (cooperative) – children interact together in complementary roles towards a common goal; this is a demanding form of play that requires children to have some theory of mind, to have mature cooperative skills; it provides a very powerful tool for learning. In collaborative play children share ideas and agendas, have the opportunity to take the lead or be led, develop negotiating skills, share and develop language, which helps them develop as a rounded person.

Gender and play

Although there are obvious physical differences between boys and girls and, some would argue, related psychological differences, the major differences between boys' and girls' behaviour are learned (refer back to Chapter 3 to review this). Gender roles are culturally determined and are learned through our interaction with others. In play children will often re-enact the roles as they perceive them – what does the 'dad' do, what does the 'mum' do in the home corner? On occasions they will 'try on' the other gender role; they will negotiate and construct with their peers how boys and girls should act. This helps the children understand their roles in the world.

Children's understanding of gender roles that lead to stereotypical behaviour, however, can have negative effects on their learning. Different kinds of play in the early years tend to support particular areas of learning. For example, domestic play and mark making to which girls are attracted, and boys are not, are particularly focused on language and emotional development, whereas construction and physical play that attract boys, but not girls, address the scientific and physical aspects of development. In later life, girls tend to be better at language and are more emotionally developed while boys are better at science and are physically more developed; this would suggest that in fact they would benefit from play in the areas they avoid. Therefore, for settings to meet children's needs effectively they need to monitor where children play and encourage them to play in all areas of the setting. This will require practitioners to think carefully about how they attract children to areas of provision, for example, through resources or adult presence. You might re-read your gender observation work from Chapter 3 at this point.

Types of play and their importance

Exploratory play

In exploratory play the child uses her senses to explore and discover all she can about the world around her. This is the first kind of play in which babies get involved. There are two stages in exploratory play, first play that answers the question what is this object, what does it do? Next, play that answers the question what can I do with this object? Although most common in early childhood, it is the kind of play seen throughout our lives whenever we come across new things or objects. This kind of play is important as it supports children's understanding of how their world works; it also supports physical development and the development of problem solving. When a child is introduced to a new material or experience he may need a period of exploratory play before he can integrate the material into other forms of play. An example of this is children's behaviour when they are first offered clay.

Heuristic play is a form of exploratory or discovery play typical of toddlers which involves activities such as filling, discarding, stacking, knocking down, selecting and manipulating in other ways. It is the kind of play parents observe when children explore the contents of cupboards, whereas in settings this play takes place with such things as treasure baskets containing natural and man-made materials. During the play children work independently and without direction, making discoveries for themselves, while adults sit quietly nearby and use the time to observe or support the child's actions.

Imaginative play

There is now much evidence that points to the importance of high-quality imaginative (pretend) play for the development of cognitive competence. Such play supports the development of areas of the brain related to metacognition, problem solving, social cognition, literacy, mathematics, and science. Therefore, where children do not have the opportunity for imaginative play, there may be negative consequences for intellectual development in the long term (Bergen 2002).

Drawing together what has been said about imaginative play we can begin to recognize its importance. In imaginative play children can go beyond the here and now; they can pretend to be someone else, to act out adult roles. This kind of play is very important because it helps children to develop their understanding of how others might think and feel (theory of mind, emotional intelligence). Crucially in imaginative play, by making one thing stand for another, the child begins to think symbolically, that is, to separate thought from actions and objects. Imaginative play develops children's problem-solving skills as it demands that the player imagines alternative scenarios, evaluates them and makes choices. In imaginative play children are constantly dealing with the concepts of 'what if' and 'what next'. In imaginative play children can take on roles and practise the cultural activities of their community; in this way they become more skilled players and come to understand the activities they see around them in society.

Figure 5.3 Imaginative play supports the development of areas of the brain related to such things as metacognition, problem solving, social cognition, literacy, mathematics and science

Physical play

Physical play, such as climbing, pushing, carrying and digging form part of most children's play and the benefits to their health and physical development are well recognized and it is this kind of play that often predominates in outdoor provision. However, physical play that is well planned, provisioned and supported can also provide excellent support for other areas of development, for example, children's sense of well-being and emotional development, their understanding of their own bodies and what they can do, their sense of space and direction as well as their social development and ability to cooperate and collaborate. One of the biggest demands on practitioners in providing good quality physical play is to offer challenge safely both in terms of the child's own safety and that of those around her. In addition to the safety checks that are routinely done, such as checking resources for damage, there are three key principles to adhere to in this respect. The first is to consider the ZPD; what can the children already do and so what challenge is just beyond that? The second is to consider how scaffolding will be provided, what support will the children need and where will it come from? Finally consideration must be given to how the activity will impact on the immediate area and the children in it (see also Chapter 8).

Play with natural materials

Play with natural materials is amongst the most rewarding experiences you can offer children. There is a wide range of natural materials that are suitable for young children to play with indoors and out, which will offer them a rich and varied experience and allow you to meet all the requirements for good quality play provision. Although not the major reason for using them, natural materials also tend to be less expensive than manufactured resources. Even basic early years provision should include: sand, water, found natural materials, clay and a garden area. Natural materials help children learn about their world and the materials that make it up; they provide opportunities to use all the senses; they are more unpredictable, unique, versatile and challenging than man-made toys. Opportunities need to be provided for children to experiment with the materials and to use the materials in combination. In some countries natural materials are the only material children have to play with; they climb trees, build dens with branches, dig in the mud and count with stones.

Figure 5.4 There is a wide range of natural materials suitable for young children to play with, indoors and out, which offer them a rich and varied experience

Creative play

While it could be argued that all play is creative, this section is about creative arts play. A culture's creative arts, such as painting, drawing, music, dance and model making, are ways of expressing ideas and feelings; they are a form of communication. In the early years setting they should retain this function rather than becoming copying and fine motor development exercises with predetermined products such as Easter cards. In their creative arts play children explore the medium, learn how it works and what they can do with it. They use it to represent ideas, to tell stories, to represent dynamic movement; they talk as they create both to themselves and to others around them. Although its main benefits are in the areas of communication and imagination, creative arts work has the potential to address all areas of development.

Outdoor play

> Young children require space, indoors and outdoors, where they can be active or quiet, and where they can think, dream and watch others (EYFS 2007: 03).

Outdoor play is now recognized as an essential part of the child's early years experience and of equal value to indoor play. The outdoors offers children space to be noisy and messy without being reprimanded, and in different group sizes without being organized by adults. The outdoors provides space to move about more freely, to dance, run, jump, skip and climb when they wish to. Children can work on a larger scale and use open-ended resources that can be used for a range of purposes, determined by the children, which can be manipulated and changed. The outdoors provides an environment different to indoors where they can experience the elements and engage and experiment with the natural world to experience textures, smells, sounds, shapes and gradients, which cannot be offered indoors. Concepts such as height and weight can be appreciated on a larger scale when engaged in physical play such as moving a wheelbarrow full of stones. Some role play about outdoor events such as fire fighting or going on holiday has greater meaning when it takes place in the outdoors. The larger space also allows mark making on a large scale. More complex and demanding collaborative play can be offered that requires groups of children to work together with challenging materials to solve problems such as constructing a den. Some children, especially boys, learn better out of doors; they behave in a more focused way; feel less inhibited and respond differently to adults. Working outdoors has a positive impact on children's emotional well-being.

Out-of-doors children become more aware of safety, of keeping themselves safe and of considering the safety of others. In the outdoors, children can find a space for themselves to be alone; they can seek solitude in a den or a quiet area of a garden. Children who have more access to the outdoors environment develop competence in operating in a larger space. They gain the ability to operate within the world safely and confidently.

The outdoor environment

Being outdoors has a positive impact on children's sense of well-being and helps all aspects of children's development.

Being outdoors offers opportunities for doing things in different ways and on different scales than when indoors.

It gives children first-hand contact with weather, seasons and the natural world

(EYFS Principles in to practice card 3.3 Enabling Environments).

Activity 5.4: Personal learning journal

You may need to tackle this activity over a number of weeks.

Purpose: To investigate the range of learning opportunities a child experiences during play in your setting.

- Observe any play situation in your setting that you feel is of good quality. Use a narrative account noting what the children do and what they say
- On a personal learning journal record sheet, note down in the first section a brief description of the context. Then analyse your findings identifying the key features of play, the learning you think took place and the learning dispositions it encouraged and record these in the second section. Then think about what you learned and complete the section. You will present these findings to the team meeting

Team meeting

- Share your findings with your group
- Listen to the other presentations and consider how they add to your understanding or challenge your perceptions (see further activity below at this point)
- Following the meeting, note the key issues that arose from the team meeting in the third section of your sheet
- Now reflect upon your ability to articulate your findings and analysis and complete the fourth section. If you complete the further activity you should take account of your feedback from the group

Further activity

Invite the team to evaluate and feed back on your analysis and understanding of the play and learning taking place during your observation.

Activity 5.5: Team meeting

- Each member of the team should take one area of learning to observe
- Watch your target child at play
- Using simple lists or adhesive notes, jot down the opportunities the child has to draw from and extend her understanding of that area of learning
- Each person should feed back to the team about the opportunities for development and learning in the area they chose. The team should then consider what this tells them about how rich the provision is in relation to opportunities for learning in each area

Activity 5.6: Team meeting

- Each member of the team should come to the meeting having reminded themselves of the statements about play in the Foundations Stage Guidance, the Early Years Foundation Stage material or the guidance/framework to which they work
- Return to the ideas map that the team constructed as part of the introductory chapter activities. In turn each member of the team should choose one item from the map of which they think they have now a better understanding, and explain it to the group and indicate where it fits in with statements in the guidance material
- Examine all areas of which you are unsure

Summary

The chapter has explored the nature of play and its role in learning. The key points made in the chapter are that:

- children's play is a cross-cultural phenomenon
- the child's right to play is enshrined in the United Nations Declaration of the Rights of the Child
- views of what counts as play vary but most agree play involves concepts of enjoyment, choice, creativity, engagement and motivation
- forms of play vary from free-flow play to playful teaching
- the stress-free nature of play allows children to explore ideas in a psychologically safe context
- play encourages high levels of motivation, concentration and sustained activity
- play supports the development of positive learning dispositions
- in play children can work at their highest level of cognitive functioning
- play allows children to learn actively, engaging the whole child
- play supports the development of skills, concepts and ideas across all areas of development

- good quality play allows children to learn through a wide range of experiences supported by knowledgeable and sensitive adults
- good quality play involves children in being creative, imaginative, making links with other things they have learned, taking the initiative, having time to develop ideas, being in control of their learning, engaging with peers and adults as partners
- as children develop, the social context of their play moves from solitary to collaborative activity
- there are many kinds of play; of particular importance to children as learners are imaginative, exploratory, creative arts, physical play, play with natural materials and outdoor play

Further reading

Corrine Hutt provides a useful taxonomy that tries to classify all types of play; this can be found in many books, for example in Moyles, J. (ed.) (1994), *The Excellence of Play*, Open University Press.

References

Bennett, N. et al. (1997), *The Quality of Pupil Learning Experiences*. London: Lawrence Erlbaum Associates.

Bergen, D. (2002), 'The role of pretend play in children's cognitive development'. *Early Childhood Research and Practice*, 4 (1), (Spring 2002).

Bruce, T. (1991), *Time to Play in Early Childhood Education*. London: Hodder and Stoughton.

Bruner, J., Jolly, A., Sylva, K. et al. (1976), *Play: Its Role in Development and Evolution*. London: Penguin.

DfES (Department for Education and Skills) (2007), 'Effective Practice: The Learning Environment', in *The Early Years Foundation Stage: Setting the Standards for Learning, Development and Care for Children from Birth to Five*. DfES.

Erikson, E.H. (1984), *Childhood and Society*. London: Paladin.

Froebel, F.W. (1887), *The Education of Man*. New York: Appleton.

Jensen, P. and H. Scott (1980), 'Beyond competition: organising play environments for co-operative and individualistic outcomes', in P.F. Wilkinson (1980), *In Celebration of Play*. London: Croom Helm.

Moyles, J. (1994), *The Excellence of Play*. Oxford University Press.

Piaget, J. (1976), 'Mastery play', in Jolly, A. and Sylva, K. (eds) (1976), *Play: Its Role in Development and Evolution*. London: Penguin.

Plato (2000), *The Republic*, Ferrari, G. R. F. (ed.). Cambridge: Cambridge University Press.

United Nations (1959) Declaration of the Rights of the Child. Available at: http://www.unhchr.ch/html/menu3/b/25.htm

Vygotsky, L. (1966), 'Play and its role in the mental development of the child', in Bruner, J., Jolly, A. and Sylva, K. (eds) (1976), *Play: Its Role in Development and Evolution*. London: Penguin.

—— (1978), *Mind in Society: The Development of Higher Psychological Processes*. Cambridge, Mass.: Harvard University Press.

Developing the Context: Making Sense of Your Setting

6

Chapter Outline

Introduction	105
Evaluation against key principles	106
The role of the practitioners in play	110
Personal development	111
Further reading	112

Introduction

The challenges for all early childhood settings in their attempt to provide effective learning through play are:

- to understand how children are learning during their play
- to be able to see what children are learning during their play
- to provide a context in which children can learn through play
- to support and extend children's learning during play
- to develop the skills and habits of reflective practice in its staff
- to motivate and enthuse all the staff about their work with children

These are challenges that require ongoing reflection and learning. The following section is an audit of practice in your setting and will focus on the team's understanding of the child and her play in your setting. All activities included in this chapter are related to team meetings or your preparation for them.

With the information you have gained from the previous chapters and activities you have already completed you should be in a position to evaluate the effectiveness of your setting in relation to the current practice, knowledge and understanding about play and the impact of your practice on children's learning through play. You should also be in a position to consider what action you should be taking at an individual and setting level to improve the quality of play.

Purpose of this chapter

The purpose of this chapter is to support you in reviewing the practice in your setting, reflecting on your personal knowledge and understanding and in doing so to help you to identify action for development.

Evaluation against key principles

Throughout this section, evaluate how well the setting is doing by noting whether the issue you are considering is a strength, acceptable or a weakness of your setting. Note down where evidence of this would be found. A key question (or questions) for each task is provided to promote discussion amongst the team or to help individual reflection.

Activity 6.1: Reviewing current practice

Key question: how well does your provision meet the criteria for good quality play?

Using the key indicators of good quality play, highlighted in Chapter 4 and reproduced below, consider the key question.

All provision for play that fulfils the purposes we have discussed above has several features in common; it allows children to:

- physically manipulate the things in their environment
- learn through all their senses
- have the opportunity to engage in active learning
- learn within a meaningful social and cultural context
- work at their own pace
- make choices and decisions that matter to them
- be immersed in their own concerns (schema)
- be totally involved
- behave spontaneously
- explore ideas, feelings and emotions safely
- pretend, be imaginative and create
- be supported by adults who know how and when to support them

Good quality play allows for effective learning when it involves:

- creative and imaginative play activities that promote thinking and its expression through different modes of representation

---

Activity 6.1 (continued)

- children making links in their learning that lead to more complex brain development
- children learning in different ways and at different rates
- children feeling secure and becoming confident learners
- children having time to explore ideas and interests in depth
- children initiating activity that promotes learning and enables them to learn from each other
- children taking control of their own learning
- the use of all the senses
- the opportunity to explore a rich range of natural and cultural artefacts
- encouragement and supportive interaction between children, their peers and the adults in the setting

As a team, identify and record what the key issues are, in relation to play opportunities in your setting, that you need to address.

Activity 6.2: Reviewing current knowledge and understanding

You will find it helpful to review the work you have done for previous chapters, for example the ideas map about play you completed, before you start this activity.

Key questions

- Does the setting have a clear vision of what good quality play looks like?
- Do all practitioners have a good understanding of how children learn during their play?
- Do all practitioners know what might influence learning and do they take it into account when working with children and planning for play?

Finally, as a team, consider what the key issues are, in relation to practitioners' knowledge and understanding of play and learning, that you need to address.

Activity 6.3: Considering the impact of your current position on the quality of the children's experience

For this section of the audit you need to reflect on what you have observed children doing and saying and consider how the provision in your setting influences their learning through play.

Key questions

- How independently do children behave?
- Are children deeply involved so that you see evidence of concentration, sustained interest and thinking, commitment to what they are doing?
- Do you see evidence of the development of positive dispositions to learning such as perseverance, curiosity, creativity and imagination?
- Are children manipulating objects, tools and materials confidently?
- Is there evidence of collaboration?
- Are children able to engage in pretence, to use their imagination, to be creative?
- Are children given opportunities to apply, practise, rehearse and repeat skills and actions?
- Is there evidence that children are pursuing their own interests and concerns?
- Do children seem to feel physically and emotionally secure?

Figure 6.1 Levels of involvement and collaboration are key indicators of good quality provision

As a team, consider what the key issues are, in relation to children's play, that you need to address.

Activity 6.4: What are the children's perceptions of their play experience?

One way of exploring your current provision is to ask the children (of course, with young babies this will not be possible and you might consider talking to parents). Getting the children's perspective may help you to be more objective and to question 'taken for granted' opinions and judgements.

Consider a range of strategies for supporting children's discussions with you, for example using photographs of the children playing as the focus. You need to get into a conversation rather than ask a series of questions but think about what you want to find out, for example:

- Do they like playing?
- What do they play?
- What do they like playing best?
- Who decides where they play?
- When do they think they can play?
- Do they play with other children?
- Do adults play with them sometimes?
- Do they think adults like playing?
- Do they think playing helps them to learn?
- What do they think they are doing if adults are not involved in their play?

Finally, as a team, consider what the information you have gathered tells you about how children see their play. Were there any surprises? Were your own judgements challenged or confirmed?

Activity 6.5: Identifying action for development

Before the team meeting, as an individual, consider all the evidence and identify areas you think need action. At the meeting share your ideas and try to come to a consensus about the setting's overall strengths and areas of weakness that need action, in relation to children's play.

The following section may help you focus on what adults are doing, which might account for what you have discovered. The following chapters will ask you to develop the work of the adults.

The role of the practitioners in play

One of the strongest indicators of a quality setting is the reflective practice of its staff. The process of reflective practice requires staff to have not only a deep understanding of how children learn and develop but also the ability to be objective, to question what they observe and what they do in the light of what they hear from other practitioners in their own communities of practice and what they read from the wider world. We have already discussed the importance of taking time to observe, listen and reflect (Chapter 1) and you have been asked to observe children playing throughout the book; now you will be asked to turn your attention to yourself and the other adults in the setting. This section will ask you to *record* the role adults take in play; your response will be *descriptive* rather than evaluative.

Using the following key questions as starting points, describe the practice in your setting and the role the practitioners take.

Values and aims

- What values and aims underpin the setting's work with play?
- Are they written down and who has access to them?
- Do adults feel they are important?
- Are the values and aims reflected in practice?
- How did you arrive at them?

Provision

Write a description of the physical environment.

- How is the physical environment of the setting organized? For example, do you have separate rooms for different types of play?
- Does the environment stay the same, and if not how are changes decided and managed?
- What are the principles and priorities that guide your decisions?
- Does the physical arrangement of the setting work well?
- What are the issues for you, the children, the rest of the staff and the parents?

Resources – equipment and consumables

- How are resources and equipment for play managed?
- How and when are they made available to the children?
- How does the setting decide what play resources it will purchase or obtain?
- Are there any issues with resources?

Planning

- How and when does the setting plan for play?
- Who is involved and what guides your decisions?
- Does the play planning work?

Interactions

- In what ways do adults interact with the children whilst they are playing?
- When do adults interact during play?
- What guides decisions about interaction?

Observation, monitoring and assessment

- How does the setting monitor how, and what, children are learning during play?
- What use is made of the information gathered by staff?
- Do you feel you are able to assess children's learning and achievement through play?

Management

- Do you feel play is managed well in the setting?
- Do staff in the setting work as a team in relation to children's play? Is everyone involved?
- What systems and procedures are there in place to monitor and enhance play? Is there a coherent plan in place to provide professional development activities for staff in relation to their understanding and use of play?

Personal development

This section asks you to reflect briefly on your own work with play, recording your thoughts in your Learning Journal.

Reviewing your current practice

Using the ideas that have emerged from your reflection on the work of the setting, think about your own work with the children. Identify your strengths and the areas you feel need developing. Consider how you might go about this.

Reviewing current knowledge and understanding

Think about your current stage of development in relation to your knowledge and understanding. You will need to consider which areas of knowledge you are still unsure about, for example. You might return to your ideas map to help you do this.

Consider the impact of your current work on the quality of the children's play experience. During the course of one day, keep a diary of what you do with children during their play, note the response you get from them and the effect your involvement has on their play. At the end of the day reflect on how far you enhanced their play and their learning. You will return to this diary in Chapter 9.

Identifying action for development

Note those things you feel confident you know and understand, those things you need to clarify and those things you are still very unsure about. Where the areas you need to clarify or are unsure of are related to the work already covered in this book, you should re-read the chapters and consider doing the additional reading. Other areas you will return to in the personal development section of Chapter 12 having completed the following chapters. Try to identify, from your reflection on your involvement with the children, times when the intervention was successful and times when you were less happy with it. What does this tell you about the skills or knowledge you need to develop? Again you will return to this in Chapter 12.

Further reading

Laevers, F., Vandenbussche, E., Kog, M. and Depondt, L. (undated), *A Process-oriented Child Monitoring System for Young Children*. Leuven: Centre for Experiential Education.

If you are interested in how you might measure the quality of provision by considering how engaged children are you may find this book of interest as it looks at ways to measure children's involvement.

Siraj-Blatchford, I., Sylva, K., Muttock, S., Gilden, R. and Bell, D. (2002), *Researching Effective Pedagogy in the Early Years*. DfES.

For a full outline of this publication see Appendix 5.

Part Three
KEY PRINCIPLES FOR DEVELOPING AND SUPPORTING PLAY

The Role of the Practitioner: Monitoring and Assessment of Children's Learning Through Play

7

Chapter Outline

Introduction	115
Defining monitoring and assessment	116
Reasons for monitoring and assessing children's play	116
Key principles for monitoring and assessing children's learning through play	118
Approaches and procedures for monitoring and assessment	122
Exemplar for assessment and recording	126
Summary, Further reading, References	132

Introduction

Monitoring and assessment is part of the observation, assessment, planning and intervention cycle. We have already discussed observation in Chapter 1 and you have carried out several methods of recording observations. This chapter will support you further by looking at how assessment builds on observation, the role of the practitioner, policy development and an alternative method for recording.

Purpose of this chapter

To help you understand:

- the importance of monitoring and assessment
- the role of the practitioner in monitoring and assessment
- the process of monitoring and assessment

Defining monitoring and assessment

Drummond defines monitoring and assessment as

> ...the ways in which, in our everyday practice, we observe children's learning, strive to understand it, and then put our understanding to good use (Drummond 2003: 13).

For the purpose of this book we have defined the elements of observation, monitoring and assessment (see Table 7.1).

Table 7.1: The elements of observation, monitoring and assessment defined for the purpose of this book

Observation	Monitoring	Assessment
Definition: A method by which we might gather information, through watching and listening, about a particular behaviour or ability	Definition: The systematic gathering of information against specic criteria to check progression and development	Definition: A review of the information gathered and evaluation of achievement. A judgement is then made about 'what next?'
Key question: Through observation we seek to answer the question, What is happening?	Key question: Through monitoring we seek to answer the question, Is what we plan to happen, actually happening?	Key question: Through assessment we look more closely and seek to answer the question, How well is something happening and what should be done next?

Reasons for monitoring and assessing children's play

Monitoring and assessment is the systematic analysis of observational information in order to make judgements about children's learning and achievement and to evaluate the play environment. It should focus on the analysis of the learning strategies children use in their play, children's learning dispositions, and progress against intended or identified learning and developmental outcomes within the context provided. The quality of learning depends on the extent to which the play environment provides stimulation, challenge and supports learning and such analysis should inform future decisions about planning and intervention.

Monitoring and assessment informs the practitioner in making decisions regarding: play provision and experiences that will build upon children's strengths and interests; progress against learning outcomes and informed and skilful interventions in the learning process.

Documented evidence from ongoing assessments can be used to track children's progress over a period of time and subsequently shared with parents, carers and other colleagues involved with the children. Play at home is also significant and therefore information from parents and carers should contribute to the assessment process, as should the children's own viewpoints on their learning. This two-way process also supports practitioners in identifying and diagnosing emerging patterns in behaviour and learning.

Observation and assessment enables practitioners to summarize learning and provide information for externally required assessments. Assessing and evaluating their own knowledge, understanding, practice and professional needs improves the practitioner's reflective skills and highlights any bias in terms of curriculum, environment, provision and children.

Case Study 7.1

The following is a case study of a practitioner using observations to deepen her understanding of a child and the subsequent changes made to the play provision in order to extend his learning.

Through her observations of John, the practitioner notices his free-flow play is largely solitary. She has kept anecdotal records but she is unsure of John's particular interests and whether it is appropriate to encourage other children to become involved with his play. She decides to monitor his play for a week to determine his particular interest, by making target child observations and continuing with anecdotal records. She tracks the provision areas in which he chooses to play and notices if other children become involved. On three occasions she chooses to work alongside John. Analysis of the information gathered leads her to the conclusion that John is interested in building bridges in a variety of learning contexts. When working alongside John using the building blocks, he copies and extends many of her ideas. Although it had previously seemed he engaged in solitary play, John listens and watches other children, using and adapting their ideas. His language demonstrates he is beginning to share his ideas and negotiate materials. Her assessment of his learning concludes that it is beyond what she originally thought and he is especially creative in construction. He also paints and draws bridges. Socially he is beginning to engage with others in order to extend his thinking. She decides to provide resources outdoors for building bridges, for example, building blocks, boxes and crates, which requires him to move from cooperative to collaborative play. She also introduces more challenging vocabulary such as span, distance, width, height, and reinforces the concepts he is beginning to explore such as stability. She provides books on bridges and stories such as 'Three Billy Goats Gruff'.

Key principles for monitoring and assessing children's learning through play

The following is a set of key principles or guidelines that will help you in setting up and writing a policy for assessment that considers process as well as outcomes.

Principle 1

There is a shared agreement and understanding amongst the practitioners of the strategies and systems in place for assessment, observation, recording, analysis and discussion and filing of information.

There needs to be an agreed policy, including guidelines for implementation, for which everyone takes ownership. Relevant to your context, it will clearly set out the what, when, by whom and how of monitoring and assessment. Any systems put in place should be realistic, adhered to and monitored.

Principle 2

Assessment focuses on the positive aspects of children's progress and within the context of their own development.

Assessment is ipsative, that is, concerned with the individual rather than making comparative judgements with other children. It should focus on achievements and the positive aspects of children's development. This will enable practitioners to interact or intervene in a way that can provide appropriate challenge or meet particular needs. Learning is mostly likely to occur in situations where children feel confident and appropriately supported. By building on their learning and developmental strengths, children will continue to be motivated and involved in their play.

Principle 3

Assessment focuses on how children learn within the play environment.

The provision of a high quality play environment or 'instructive learning environment' (Siraj-Blatchford et al., 2002) will enable the practitioner to assess children operating at their 'highest level'. Assessment will include judgements about how children engage with tools and materials and the way in which they control and manipulate their play surroundings. It takes account of the type of play in which they engage, the language they use and thought processes they display when engaging with others, plus their ability to stay motivated, concentrate and persevere.

Principle 4

Assessment builds on observation, informs future learning intentions and makes judgements against outcomes.

From the observations made there will be a wealth of information regarding individual children and their learning through play. Assessment involves the analysis of these observations, making judgements and using the information to decide on an appropriate form of intervention. This includes discussion with colleagues, parents and children. The information is also used to measure progress against outcomes. Assessment deepens the practitioner's understanding of children's learning and can inform their shared values on play.

Principle 5

Assessment can be made through interaction, which is the most powerful form of assessment.

Collaborating with children in pursuing their interests gives the practitioner a wonderful insight into children's thinking. Observing behaviours is not enough; we need to give children the opportunity to show understanding and communicate with us in a situation where they remain in control. Sayeed and Guerin (2000) talk about 'play based assessment', which consists of observation and 'participatory play' where the practitioner assesses whilst being involved in the child's everyday play. The adult takes on the combined role of 'assessor, participator and mediator', with the aim of looking at children's understanding, learning potential and patterns. The degree to which the practitioner needs to engage or support the children provides an indication of what intervention may be required in the future. The role of mediator may involve, for example, helping children to decide upon a particular focus for their play; using questioning, especially 'how' questions; discussing previous learning and applying it to a new situation; and challenging children's comments and answers to questions, even when correct, as this assesses their ability to reflect upon their ideas and strategies.

Through the different functions of interaction, assessments can be made. This is dealt with in more depth in Chapter 9 but may involve the practitioner in:

- modelling their own thinking by wondering aloud ('I wonder what would happen if…') to see how this takes the children's thinking forward
- listening to, and assessing, the children's use of language in expressing their ideas and intentions
- engaging with a group of children who are playing in order to assess their ability to collaborate and cooperate with each other
- providing technical vocabulary relating to a subject and listening for its use
- looking at children's application of skills and knowledge
- identifying whether, and to what extent, a particular influence is impacting upon a child's learning and development

Figure 7.1 The practitioner assesses while being involved in the child's everyday play

Principle 6

Assessment of children's learning and learning behaviour is at the same time an evaluation of the provision.

Where there is high quality provision and an environment that allows children to operate at their 'highest level', then practitioners will be able to assess the children's skills, knowledge, thought processes, interests, social interactions and attitudes to learning. When observing and interacting with children, practitioners should be evaluating the extent to which the environment facilitates involvement and allows children to demonstrate their highest level of operation. In addition, provision areas need to be evaluated for curriculum coverage; does each area of provision cover the six areas of learning? For example, if children are counting, matching and sorting cups and saucers, as they lay the table in role play, are there enough resources to extend counting and in a range of colours, sizes, and other types for classification? In other words, high quality provision facilitates high quality learning, which allows for thorough assessment.

Principle 7

The thoughts and viewpoints of all practitioners, children, parents and carers are respected and valued as part of the assessment process.

The Curriculum Guidance for the Foundation Stage states that:

> Parents are children's first and most enduring educators. When parents and practitioners work together in early years settings, the results have a positive impact on the child's development and learning. Therefore, each setting should seek to develop an effective partnership with parents. A successful partnership needs a two-way flow of information, knowledge and expertise (DfES, 2000: 9).

Sharing assessments with parents and carers gives them an insight into their children's learning. It helps them see how the everyday things children do have a purpose; that every experience is a learning opportunity and it encourages them to see value in children's play. By emphasizing the positive aspects of children's learning they can share in children's achievements, be involved in their interests and have a greater understanding of the role of play. Contributions from parents regarding children's interests, skills and needs should be positively sought through a range of opportunities, and used to support judgements about children's future learning experiences.

Sharing assessments with children gives them positive messages about their learning. It is important that children feel valued and that their viewpoints are respected. Discussing achievements, and the aspects of play they enjoy, supports children in reflecting on and self-evaluating their learning and ultimately taking responsibility for it. Discussing learning with a group of children supports them in understanding how they can learn from each other; for example, saying why something is good, talking about a particular aspect of their play, asking questions about what they are doing and thinking and providing them with feedback related to their learning. Using photographs, models, drawings, may be a useful way of supporting the discussion.

Principle 8

Children are allocated a key practitioner who builds up a deep relationship with the child and an understanding of his learning and development.

A deep relationship will enable the key practitioner to know the child, to understand his learning across all aspects of the play provision and within different social contexts. They will gather information from a range of sources, including parents and colleagues, to build up a picture of the child. This will support the practitioner in creating appropriate provision and drawing meaningful, well-informed conclusions for external, summative assessment purposes.

Approaches and procedures for monitoring and assessment

The following is an outline of the approaches and procedures you need to consider for developing your strategy for monitoring and assessment and its implementation.

Observation and assessment methods need to be matched to the purpose identified. For example, the best methods of monitoring the use of a resource might be a time sample or event sample. Assessment through interaction might be the most appropriate method of identifying children's learning strategies. For making judgements about learning processes, a narrative, anecdotal or learning story may be more appropriate.

The recording method you choose needs to be manageable and give you the required information; so again, fitness for purpose should be considered. This decision-making process can be seen as a continuum from choosing an informal non-recording method because the assessment is made and acted on immediately, through choosing specific methods, to summative assessments, which you are required to record on external curriculum profiles (see Table 7.2).

Table 7.2 The recording continuum

Informal non-recorded	Anecdotal records	Sampling	Narratives	Learning stories	Summative profiles

Informal ◄──────────────────────────────────────► Formal

Establishing the clarity of role for each practitioner, especially the role of the key practitioner in the monitoring and assessment process, involves deciding who will do what, when and how. It will also include the review and evaluation of any teaching and other forms of interaction with children. Good practice will involve team meetings with a consistent format and an agenda to ensure there is shared feedback about children's play and learning.

Decisions need to be made regarding the storage and accessibility of information. This includes information gathered on a daily basis (such as Post-its, anecdotal notes, record sheets) as well as the completion of portfolios showing significant achievements, learning journeys and children's progress against outcomes. Some of this information will inform planning (long-term foci and provision, outlines for the week and daily activities).

Each setting will develop its own way of sharing and celebrating achievements with parents and carers, other practitioners and children. This may include regular formal meetings to discuss assessments, regular opportunities to review portfolios, informal discussions, open days, adult involvement in the day-to-day routines and wall-mounted displays.

Feedback to children about their learning should be embedded in the practitioner's intervention in their play, through photographs, experiences and sharing children's work.

There needs to be consideration of how assessments can inform future learning on a long- and short-term basis. Methods of recording should provide opportunity for evaluations about the learning environment and provision. Assessments will need to inform provision, resources and planning as described in Chapters 8 and 10.

Figure 7.2 Using every opportunity to assess children's learning. Playful teaching and assessment

Activity 7.1: Team meeting

Purpose: To understand the process of developing a policy for monitoring and assessing children's play.

All practitioners in the setting should be involved so they have ownership of the monitoring and assessment process. Several meetings might be needed for you to complete this exercise.

Consider the following:

- a rationale
- aim
- goals or statements of intent
- guidelines
- review

For each of the key areas below discuss your current practice and how it might be improved. Pool your thoughts in note format. Decide upon a lead person who is responsible for writing up each section.

A rationale

A rationale is the overarching reason or underlying principle for why we observe, monitor and assess. It is useful to draw on national policy and/or research, and a relevant quote may be used as an introduction to the rationale.

For example: In Dingly Dell Nursery observation and assessment is the means by which we can understand children's development and learning, plan future intervention and evaluate.

> Ongoing assessment is an integral part of the learning and development process. Providers must ensure that practitioners are observing children and responding appropriately to help them make progress from birth towards the early learning goals (DfES, 2007: 16).

Aim

An aim is a short statement that sets out in general your setting's intention for observation, monitoring and assessment of play. It is based on your values and beliefs.

For example: In our setting we aim for practitioners to be effective in observing, monitoring and assessing children's learning through play in order to provide a well-planned play environment in which children can operate at their 'highest level'. We value the contributions of parents and carers and understand the importance of children recognizing their own achievements.

Activity 7.1 (continued)

Goals or statements of intent

These are more specific goals and detail your intentions for your practice.

Use bullet points to list your goals.

Ask the following questions to help you write your statements:

- Why do we observe children at play?
  e.g. we will observe children at play because..........
- Why do we monitor play?
  e.g. we will monitor play to ensure..........
- Why do we assess for future learning?
- Why do we summarize learning?
- Why do we diagnose learning?
- Why do we plan for the monitoring and assessment of play?
- Why do we involve parents?
- Why do we involve the children in assessing their learning through play?

Guidelines for how you intend to achieve your goals

Guidelines indicate how you intend to observe, monitor and assess children's play. Use bullet points and the following questions to help you write your statements. These statements may later be used as a checklist for monitoring:

- What are we observing, monitoring and assessing when children are playing?
- Which methods will we use for observing and assessing children's play?
- When will observations and assessments take place and by whom?
- How will we record, store, access and share with colleagues our observations and assessments of children's learning through play?
- How will we involve the children in the process?
- What structured opportunities will practitioners have to (a) discuss, (b) reflect, (c) implement any decisions?
- What is the role of the key practitioner?
- Are there key criteria for discussion in team meetings for the key practitioner to follow in order to consider all aspects of the assessment process?
- What training is in place to enable practitioners to develop their skills in observation and assessing?
- How will we gain contributions from parents/carers to the observation and assessment process?
- When and how will we share assessments with parents/carers?

Activity 7.1 (continued)

Review of the policy

Your policy should be reviewed on a regular basis as part of monitoring practice. You should outline the following:

- When you will review the policy
- How you will evaluate effectiveness
- From where and from whom will you gather information regarding effectiveness
- Any changes to the policy, what, when and by whom
- Further review date

After the meetings your lead person needs to write up each section.

Further activity

Additionally, the group will take each of the goals and bullet points and carry out a mapping exercise against the eight key principles for monitoring and assessing children's learning through play, discussed earlier in this chapter. This will ensure coverage of important elements in the process. Ask yourselves is there anything you need to add or change?

Then refine your policy and present to the full team at your next meeting.

Activity 7.2: Personal learning journal

Complete a personal learning journal record sheet. In the first section briefly describe this activity and your role in writing the policy.

In the second section reflect on your contribution to the policy-writing process, your involvement and the extent to which you could offer ideas. In the third section decide what action you will take next in terms of policy implementation and your role in the team. Finally, evaluate any implementation by considering how well it worked. If you led this activity then reflect on your leadership and management capability.

Exemplar for assessment and recording

Table 7.3 is an example of a pro forma for assessment. It is one way in which the child's learning can be recorded. It is based on the New Zealand Te Whariki Early Years Curriculum (Ministry of Education 1996) and the learning stories of Margaret Carr (Carr 2001). Its aim is to encourage you to think about children's involvement in the assessment and planning process. It is a complex recording method but one that can give a wealth of information regarding a group or an individual's learning, progress against learning and developmental outcomes or an activity. It will become easier to implement when it is embedded in practice. There are three parts to the assessment method. First, it requires you to observe and photograph children in their play, consider the aspects of learning that you observed and decide what action to take next. Next, it requires you to share the photographs with the children, and encourage them to tell you what they were thinking and what they think should happen next in their play. Finally, you consider all the information, and taking the children's viewpoints as well as your own, decide on action.

This method can be used:

- as a summative assessment, for example each term with an individual or a group of children
- for assessing a particular play activity that is very rich and enduring
- for assessing a child or group of children who are making significant progress or about whom you have concerns

A guide to using the pro forma Table 7.3

Photographs: These should be annotated and may be:

- of one incident or aspect of learning
- a sequence of events based upon a child's particular interest pursued in different provision
- a series showing how a group of children develop an idea

Prompts: The prompts are to help you think about all aspects of children's learning when observing and making your comments: interests, skills and knowledge, thinking processes, social engagement, attitudes to learning.

Practitioner observation: This is a narrative of your observation relating to the photographs and answers the question, 'What is happening here?'

Reflection: A judgement is made based upon analysis of the narrative and then a consideration of what comes next.

What next?: A decision about how the children's learning will be supported and the course of intervention you will make.

Children's viewpoint: This is a narrative based upon what the children tell you in answer to the questions: 'What is happening here?'; 'What were you thinking about?' You will need to note down what they say.

What do you think should happen next?: This is where you ask the children what they would like to happen next. How would they like to take their learning forward?

Conclusions: In this section you are evaluating children's learning, the play provision, the curriculum and yourselves i.e. your interpretation, judgement, values and assumptions.
  You need to:

- consider what you think should happen next according to what the children say
- discuss this at a team meeting or with a key practitioner if you are not that person
- consider balancing the interests and wishes of the children with what you consider to be an appropriate way forward
- take action: how will you next challenge the children?

In this section note down how you will provide some level of challenge and take the children's thinking forward. Think also about curriculum outcomes the children may have achieved and which could be addressed.

Activity 7.3: Personal learning journal

Purpose:

- To understand the contribution that monitoring and assessment can make to identifying and meeting the needs of individual children
- To understand the value of involving the children in the assessment process

Activity:

- Photocopy Table 7.3 (either onto one A3 sheet of paper or two A4 sheets side by side)
- Choose a small group of children who are engaged in play together or an individual who is playing
- Take photographs of significant aspects of their play. Alongside this, make a narrative observation or observations. (You may wish to do this by recording on sticky labels and writing up later or writing straight on the pro forma in the 'What was happening here?' Practitioner observation column. It will depend upon your purpose for use.)
- Stick the photographs onto the pro forma. You may also want to annotate underneath them

Analysis:

- Use the photographs and your narrative to enter key aspects of children's learning into the 'Prompts' column
- Use the photographs, the 'Prompts' column and your narrative to reflect upon significant learning and complete the 'Reflection' box
- Reach a conclusion, consider what action you will take and write this in the 'What next?' box

Table 7.3 Assessment pro forma

Date of assessment period.................................

Contextual information.................................

Photograph(s)	Prompts	Practitioner observation
	Interest	
	Skills Knowledge	
	Thought processes	
	Social engagement including language	
	Attitudes	
	Reflection What significant learning is happening?	What next?

Name(s) of children involved.................................

Children's viewpoint	Conclusion
Tell me what is happening here? What were you thinking about?	
What do you think should happen next?	ACTION – How will you next challenge the children?

Activity 7.4: Personal learning journal

At an appropriate moment draw the children together to look at the chosen photographs and say 'Tell me what was happening here', then later 'Tell me what you were thinking.' You may want to tape-record this interview with the children. At this stage you may keep the photographs on the computer or interactive whiteboard for ease of discussion. Write their narrative in the 'Children's viewpoint' column. Finally, when you feel the children have explained enough, say: 'What do you think should happen next?'

Conclusion:

- Review and analyse your thoughts against the children's.
- What did you notice?
- How were they the same or different?
- Were there any surprises?

Consider:

- What have you learned about the children's learning as individuals and as a group?
- What have you learned about the play provision?
- What have you learned in terms of learning and developmental outcomes?
- What have you learned about yourself?
- What will you do next for these children? How will you challenge them?

Activity 7.5: Team meeting

Discuss your findings and your considerations with other colleagues and together reconsider what action to take based upon your thoughts and the children's thoughts. There should be a level of realistic challenge in how you adapt the play in order to take the children's learning forward.

Evaluation

Discuss the following:

- The usefulness and practicalities of this method
- How and when you might use this method in the day-to-day operation of your setting
- How you might put this together with other information regarding children's learning
- How you might share the learning with parents and carers and the children

Activity 7.6: Personal learning journal

Complete a personal learning journal record sheet. In the first section briefly describe the activity and the context in which the observation took place. In the next section review the observations you made and reflect upon your ability to identify children's dispositions when playing, for example, motivation, concentration, perseverance, communication and contribution to the group. Return to Chapter 2 and re-read the section on learning dispositions and child involvement. See also the further study section at the end of this chapter. Think about the quality of the provision and the children's activity related to the observation by considering the extent to which it allowed the children to be fully engaged and to demonstrate these dispositions as well as skills and knowledge. (Provision will be covered in more detail in Chapter 8.) In the third section consider what action you will take to further help you in observing and understanding children's dispositions to learning. In the fourth section evaluate this action in terms of your ability and confidence in observing children's approaches to learning.

Activity 7.7: Personal learning journal

Using a personal learning journal record sheet, briefly describe the implementation of this method of assessment. In the second section reflect on and analyse your understanding of the purpose and usefulness of this method and how well you implemented it. Read about and review other methods. Talk to colleagues about their experiences of assessment. Refine your thinking in terms of previous methods of assessment used, your understanding of the process and what you have learned about your skills in making assessments. In the third section your action is to decide three things you will do differently in the future to improve the quality of the assessments you make and how you use the information to improve children's play and learning. Monitor your implementation of these three action points. In the fourth section evaluate your action points by asking what worked well and what did not.

If you are a manager, consider the value of this assessment method to the improvement in the quality of play in your setting and how you will implement it. Add this to your personal learning journal entry.

Summary

This chapter should have raised your awareness of how assessment builds on observation and provides information to support judgements about children's future learning and the quality of the play environment.

Your policy for assessing children's learning through play provides you with a set of principles that should guide your practice. You have been presented with a particular method for assessing the whole child within a social context. You should now work through Chapters 8, 9 and 10 in order to fully understand how assessment informs provision, intervention and planning.

Further reading

Broadhead, P. (2004), *Early Years Play and Learning: Developing Social Skills and Cooperation*. London: Routledge Falmer.

Carr, M. (2001), *Assessment in Early Childhood Settings: Learning Stories*. London: Paul Chapman.

Claxton, G. (2000), 'A Sure Start for an uncertain world'. Transcript of lecture. *Early Education*. Spring 2000.

   Claxton talks about children of the future needing 'learnacy' and proposes four elements of a toolkit for learning: immersion in experience, imagination, intuition, and intellect. He also talks about children developing a 'learning temperament' (persistence, playfulness and conviviality) to equip them for the future.

DfES (2007), *Statutory Framework and Practice Guidance for the Foundation Stage: Setting the Standards for Learning, Development and Care for Children from Birth to Five*. DfES.

   These documents set out the statutory framework and the practice guidance for the foundation stage, which ensures children of 0–5 achieve the five Every Child Matters outcomes of staying safe, being healthy, enjoying and achieving, making a positive contribution, and achieving economic well-being. It sets out the requirements for learning and development and welfare for children in maintained and non-maintained schools, independent schools and with registered childcare providers. Each of the areas of learning and development in appendix 2 of the guidance contains a section on observation and assessment, entitled Look, listen and note, which gives guidelines of what to look for.

References

Carr, M. (2001), *Assessment in Early Childhood Settings: Learning Stories*. London: Paul Chapman.

DfES (2000), *Curriculum Guidance for the Foundation Stage*. London: QCA.

DfES (2007), 'Statutory framework for the foundation stage', in *The Early Years Foundation Stage: Setting the Standards for Learning, Development and Care for Children from Birth to Five*. London: QCA.

Drummond, M. J. (2003), *Assessing Children's Learning.* 2nd edn. London: David Fulton.

Ministry of Education (1996), *Te Whariki: Early Childhood Curriculum.* Wellington, New Zealand: Learning Media Limited.

Sayeed, Z. and Guerin, E. (2000), *Early Years Play: A Happy Medium for Assessment and Intervention.* London: David Fulton.

Siraj-Blatchford, I., Sylva, K., Muttock, S., Gilden, R. and Bell, D. (2002), *Researching Effective Pedagogy in the Early Years* (REPEY). DfES.

8 The Learning Environment: Provision and Resources

Chapter Outline

Introduction	134
Why is the physical learning environment important?	135
What makes a quality play environment?	137
Planning provision areas	146
Summary, Jargon explained, References	152

Introduction

Thinking about the 'ecology' of the play context can help us to appreciate the interrelationship of different elements of the context, such as ethos, adult interaction and children's backgrounds, and their impact on the quality of the child's play experience. In this interrelated system each element influences others and so can determine the quality of the whole context for learning. The physical environment element is no exception.

If environments are to be effective in supporting learning, they must provide a context where children have the motivation and the opportunity to take the lead and engage actively in their own learning. The 'Researching Effective Pedagogy in the Early Years' (REPEY) project (Siraj-Blatchford et al. 2002) indicated the key aspects of practice that led to the most positive outcomes for children. One of the factors that they identified was the quality of the environment; they found good outcomes for children where there was 'the provision of instructive learning environments and routines'. They argue that 'where young children have freely chosen to play within an instructive learning environment, adult interventions may be especially effective'.

Instructive learning environments consist of both the intellectual and the physical context in which children play. Chapter 9, which covers interaction, considers the intellectual context; this chapter focuses on the physical environment and draws from previous more theoretical chapters on learning and play. It will look at the organization and provisioning of the indoor and outdoor learning environment, offer a framework for quality resourcing and consider some aspects of health and safety.

Purpose of this chapter

To help you:

- understand the importance of a well-planned and managed learning environment
- understand how provision can affect learning
- understand the need to plan provision areas with possible or intended learning/developmental outcomes in mind
- explore strategies for enhancing and evaluating play provision

Why is the physical learning environment important?

Environments are not simply spaces to work or play; they also send out messages about the kinds of activities that will or can go on, how valued people feel and how important they are. The physical environment can support the activities that go on there or can hinder them. In an educational context, learning is the major activity and so questions about the quality of the environment will focus on how well it supports learning and learning activities. 'Instructive learning environments' have embedded within their physical provision opportunities for children to learn. It is therefore not enough to think of the space in simple terms, for example is it clean and is it safe? Although these are important considerations, not only for health and safety reasons but also for the confidence children gain from feeling safe, we need also to think about how stimulating and challenging are the environments.

As the REPEY research (Siraj-Blatchford et al. 2002) clearly shows, the potential of freely chosen play to enhance learning relies on the quality of the learning environment.

Activity 8.1: Personal learning journal

Purpose: To evaluate and analyse children's independent play in a resource area.

This activity asks you to make observations of current provision areas; it has several parts and may need to be tackled over two or three weeks.

Choose a provision area that you think works well.

You need to choose an area that can be made available to the same set of children over a period of time.

Activity 8.1 (continued)

Activity A

Observe two children playing freely with the range of materials and tools. Try to observe for at least 15 minutes on both occasions.

Observe what they do and say and make notes; in particular note the following:

- How the children approach the task (including how they planned what they were going to do)
- How the children use the resources
- What the children say
- How the children interact
- How the children tackle problems and challenges

Observation should be at a distance, but where you can hear (or you may like to set up a video). The children will need uninterrupted time. Interact with the children only if they approach you. Respond to children's questions in a way that reassures them rather than giving ideas.

Afterwards ask the children to talk to you about what they did and to explain their perception of the activity. You might like to photograph what was made.

Activity B

Reflect on your observation. You should think about what you observed and how you would answer these key questions:

- What learning happened?
- What other resources would have helped the learners?
- What did you learn about the children's use of the resources?
- What did you learn about the children's use of language?
- What influenced the play other than the resources?
- What knowledge, skills, attitudes and concepts did their observable behaviour suggest they were thinking about?

Further activity: Using the relevant key characteristics of good quality play identified in Chapter 5, evaluate the quality of the play you observed.

Activity C

Using the National Curriculum, Early Years Foundation Stage documents, or whichever framework you work to, try to identify the coverage of areas of learning throughout all your observations.

Activity 8.1 (continued)

Team meeting:

As a team share what you observed and the conclusions you came to. Your discussion should be based upon the key questions in Activity B.

Further activity:

Evaluate the quality of the play across all the observations.

Figure 8.1 The pre-school should provide a rich and varied environment for mark making

What makes a quality play environment?

There are 12 key principles.

Principle 1

Environments should be designed to support the play activities you anticipate children will become involved in at a developmentally appropriate level.

The first stage in planning the play environment is to ask four key questions:

- What kind of play do our children find engaging?
- What will children be able to do in this space?
- What learning potential does the environment have?
- How will the adults work with the children?

Principle 2

Planning the environment should ensure a balance and range of play experiences.

Initial ideas should be carefully evaluated in terms of the range of play experiences they will provide. The most obvious classifications are such things as role play, sand play, and construction. These, of course, can be further refined, for example: role play – home area, outdoor role play, puppets; sand play – dry and wet; construction – wooden blocks, Lego, large outdoor construction. When this is done, however, what we have is a list of kinds of activities; what is needed now is a consideration of what this represents in terms of learning opportunities. For example, what opportunities are there for children to become engaged with mathematical thinking; to work collaboratively; to solve problems; to explore how they feel; to use language for different purposes; to engage in physical learning; to engage with the full curriculum out of doors? How will the provision support the development of learning dispositions such as curiosity, concentration and persistence? How inclusive will the provision be; will boys' and girls' interests be met; will there be good quality opportunities for children with special needs?

Principle 3

Good quality play opportunities should be provided outdoors as well as indoors.

It is well established that the provision of outdoor play opportunities is important to children's development and learning. The Statutory Framework for the Early Years Foundation Stage stipulates that settings should provide outdoor space for play or take children on outings on a daily basis (p. 34). Access to outdoor provision, which offers children the same play opportunities as they have indoors, is what all settings should aspire to. For example, sand play outdoors offers an opportunity to work on a much larger scale and to provide a sand pit the children can get into; this allows them to experience sand in a different way, using larger resources. The outdoor environment offers great opportunities for play. There are some activities that are better or can only occur outside, for example, only out of doors can children experience the weather, fly kites, build snowmen and splash in puddles. Some children work better outside; this seems especially true of boys. This means that outdoor play must be as carefully planned, resourced and supported as indoor play and wherever possible be available to the children on a continuous basis.

Figure 8.2 Good quality play opportunities should be provided outdoors: small but permanent resources need to be chosen for their potential to support learning (principles 3 and 7)

Principle 4

Provision should be flexible and allow children to invent, explore, create and re-visit learning.

Adult planning is essential in any setting, but children need opportunities to develop their own ideas, construct their own learning, and pursue their own concerns and interests. For example, whilst the adults might think that a doll's house would be good for developing small-world play about children's lives at home, a model building that children can convert into whatever they wish, a hospital, shop or palace, for example, will meet their needs much better. Pat Broadhead's work (Broadhead 2003) with theme-free role-play areas, which provided basic materials such as cardboard boxes and sheets of fabric, demonstrated how rich is the resulting play, how independently the children work and how high the levels of problem solving become. Children need freedom to be able to alter space and resources in order to meet their own play needs.

Principle 5

Thought should be given to allocation of space; the relationship of areas to each other; other significant physical features of the room and the delineation and demarcation of areas for different activities.

Creating provision areas for particular types of activities, such as construction and painting, allows practitioners to gather all the resources that might be used in that type of activity together where they are easily accessible to them and the children. It allows for activities to be sited in appropriate areas of the room and it also helps children make decisions about where they want to go and play.

Where provision areas are sited is an issue of both practical expediency and function. Thought must again be given to what children will do in the area and how the area relates to things such as thoroughfares or wash basins. When deciding where to put a painting table, for example, having the wash basin nearby is obviously advisable but you might also consider having it close to the junk-modelling area as children often wish to paint their models.

How much space you allow for each kind of play will depend very much on how much space you have, but two other issues need consideration: what the ideal number of children for that kind of play is and how much space the play will take up. If, for example, you wish children to have the opportunity to develop collaborative play in the construction area with the wooden blocks, you will need a relatively large space, whereas a drawing or mark-making area can be as small as a two-person table. Remember to consider the need of the adult to become part of the play.

When considering the demarcation of areas it is important to keep in mind the function of the demarcation. Enclosing areas with shelving, for example, will serve two purposes: it will allow you to store all the material the children may need close by and will allow children to work without the interruption of through traffic. Some visual barrier around areas can help children concentrate for longer periods; children are disturbed more by visual disturbance than by noise. Moreover, it will help them make choices about the kind of play in which they wish to become engaged. On the other hand, surrounding the area completely with screens will prevent the children from benefiting from what they might see others doing and barriers that are too high will stop adults observing the play.

Principle 6

Structural or large equipment (such as a water tray) should be chosen with care and with consideration both for the quality of the physical object, its potential for learning and the room it will take up and the use that will be made of it.

Large permanent pieces of equipment, such as water trays, will get a lot of use; they are expensive but you need to buy the best quality you can afford. It is worth remembering that whilst quality includes the quality of materials and construction it also includes how much play potential the equipment has. Generally speaking, the more the equipment is particularized to set scenarios and the more it restricts what it can be used for, the less potential there is and the fewer opportunities there will be created for children's imagination and invention. For example, a climbing frame that is built as a fort may seem very attractive at first to the children but it influences the play that goes on and restricts children's own thoughts and initiatives.

Health and safety is less of a problem if equipment is bought from reputable retailers, but you still need to consider health and safety in relation to its appropriateness for the age group, where it will be sited and how it will be used in your setting. There are obvious things such as not placing climbing equipment near to railings, not putting activities that involve water on flooring which becomes slippery when wet, but other dangers do not present themselves until you think about how the equipment will be used.

Principle 7

Small but permanent resources also need to be of good quality and chosen for their potential to support learning; quality rather than quantity should guide choice.

Quality and flexibility are again the key principles when thinking about small resources. Construction materials are a prime example of the kinds of choice we should be making. A set of good quality plain wooden blocks that come in different sizes and geometric shapes and that have a mathematical relationship to each other are expensive but they have enormous potential for creative and mathematical play. They can be built into anything the child wants, such as cars or telephones, but their uses are limited only by the child's imagination. On the other hand, a set that comes with object indicators printed on them, such as a petrol pump or a clock, limits their use; those that do not have a mathematical relationship do not offer children the opportunity to see relationships and to build up their mathematical knowledge. The same applies to interlocking blocks such as Lego; wheels, windows and doors are fine but buying sets that can be made into only one scenario is very limiting.

Another key category of small permanent resources are the accessories that allow play to be enhanced, for example: for the construction and wet sand areas – small figures, vehicles and animals; for water and dry sand – funnels, clear plastic tubing and containers; and for the garden area – magnifiers, trowels and gardening gloves. Again, you need good quality robust materials that are of an appropriate size. As a rule, equipment should be small versions of adult equipment or adult equipment, rather than 'toy' versions. For example, sharp but rounded-end scissors are safer than the blunter 'children's' versions. This is because the effort required to cut through anything, other than thin paper, is not only frustrating for the child but also means that the pressure they need to put on the scissors will result in a nasty nip should they get their fingers in between the blades.

You might think of colour coordination of resources to assist in clearing up and adding to the aesthetic appearance of the areas but this is a secondary consideration. For example, using all one colour for each area.

Principle 8

The management and planning of additional resources should take account of children's current concerns and learning as well as adult planned experiences.

When the environment is set up with play areas and basic equipment, this becomes the child's 'workshop' where her tools for learning are set out ready for use. One of the adult's roles is to enhance the environment on a regular basis in order to meet the children's current learning needs. These needs will be identified through reflection, as a team, on information gathered through observation of play, periods of interaction or direct requests from the children.

Enhancement could be simply to add a small piece of equipment to an area, for example, adding a pair of scales to the malleable materials table in response to an observation that children have become interested in heavy and light. It could involve the addition of significant amounts of extra material such as lots of different wheels and wheeled vehicles when you notice that a group of children are in a rotational schema. On occasions you may need to completely restructure an area, for example, changing the role-play area to a garage after a visit to the local garage has stimulated a great interest in 'mending cars' play. To be effective these changes must be timely so settings do need to build up a stock of enhancement materials. Some settings have theme boxes for the role-play area; experience will tell you what children might become interested in and you can prepare in good time; on other occasions children's interest will take you by surprise!

Figure 8.3 Themed boxes for enhancing outdoor play

Principle 9

Choices made because of limitations in terms of space should be carefully thought through; your understanding of children's learning, your curriculum intentions *and* evidence from observation of children playing should guide choice.

The temptation with limited space is to rotate activities frequently, even daily, in order to offer all kinds of play across the week. This can be counter productive because it does not allow children to develop their skills and ideas and it discourages them from making plans about what they might do next session. Although, as we know, the human brain thrives on variety, being constantly bombarded with new things does not give the child sufficient time to construct deep understanding.

Where space is limited, choice of activities should be made on the quality and richness of the play and what it offers the child; how many ways can the child use the material; what does your observation tell you about the learning dispositions it encourages; how well does it enable sustained shared thinking; can the same learning experience be offered in another play activity?

Where money is limited, buying expensive equipment, such as blocks, can be balanced out by using everyday objects that are inexpensive or even free such as large cardboard boxes, sand, recycled fabrics and found materials for the modelling area. Avoid expensive 'toy' versions of things and get the real thing; don't duplicate unnecessarily: for example, how many table games do you really need?

Principle 10

Resources should be stored in such a way that children can get (most of) what they need without an adult's help *and* return it to the correct place.

We know that self-initiated and self-managed play is of particular value in children's learning. One of the keys to developing such play is to facilitate the children's own management of play materials by allowing free and easy access to resources. This also has the added benefit that adults are then able to spend less time managing resources and more time observing and working with the children.

(i) Store resources as near to where they will be used as possible

Generally, if children are to make informed choices they need to be able to see what is available from where they are working. Having resources at hand cuts down possible distraction from the play when a child has to travel across the room for materials.

(ii) Store resources at a height that allows children to access them safely

This is an issue not only of visual access to what is available but also of health and safety. As a general rule nothing should be stored above the shoulder height of the smallest children who will be accessing the material. Where there are rooms with babies and very young children, you need to consider this issue carefully.

Figure 8.4 Resources should be stored in such a way that children can access them easily

(iii) Store resources where they are visible

This will allow the children to make choices, to know what is available to them and to see where resources should be returned. Seeing resources might also stimulate thinking and generate ideas. Purpose-built shelving, hooks for hanging equipment and storage boxes on the floor are the ideal solutions to the problem of visibility, but just taking doors off cupboards can serve the same purpose. Beware, however, of large boxes or deep shelves that mean lots of resources are jumbled together; this results in only the top or front objects being visible and makes tidying away too difficult for the children.

(iv) Store resources in the quantities that will be needed during one session – replenish at the end of the session

There are good reasons why we should present resources in the quantities that will be required for one session. First, especially with consumables such as paint, glue or even felt pens, it avoids waste. Second, children can handle small quantities more easily than large quantities both in terms of weight and manoeuvrability. For example, in the paint area children can dispense their own powder paint if you decant it into small tubs; if they get the process a little wrong and the water ends up in the paint pot, not much is wasted but it has allowed them to be independent. Third, it cuts down on cost and allows you to offer more choice, for example, instead of thirty paint brushes of the same size, four brushes of three different sizes is quite enough. And finally it will encourage children to tidy up as they go along.

(v) Store resources using a system that helps children put things back where they belong – small boxes with photographs of the contents, silhouettes of the object painted on shelves or underneath hooks

There are good management and educational reasons for this. First, it allows you more time during the session to involve yourself with the children's learning and at the end of the session to meet with colleagues to review and plan. Second, as well as being a good work habit to develop, managing the end of your activity yourself develops independence, a sense of agency and control. Third, the process of tidying up can have learning opportunities embedded within it, for example, matching, counting, ordering and cooperating. When this is first introduced the children will need encouragement and support but when it is established the older children can do the mentoring of the new children. With very young children, the process of tidying resources away should be modelled with accompanying dialogue from the very start.

Principle 11

The aesthetics and physical comfort of the environment should be considered.

Research in the workplace, as well as the classroom, has shown that the aesthetic quality of our environment impacts on our self-esteem and our feeling of comfort and sense of being valued. This applies to the children and to the adult team.

Before we can learn well, we need to feel comfortable and safe. Therefore, practitioners need to attend to such issues as temperature and how comfortable the room is for children and for adults.

We have looked at the importance of the senses in learning and how the practitioner can use multi-sensory learning to good effect, but if the environment itself causes sensory overload then children will not be able to distinguish more subtle sensory input. It is a good idea to get down to the level of a child sometimes and experience the setting from their viewpoint.

Principle 12

Display should be used to enhance and communicate about play.

All display should serve a purpose. In relation to play there are four particularly important functions it can serve.

First, it supports the children's play, for example the materials you or the children put on the wall in role-play areas to create the appropriate environment such as diagrams of teeth at the 'dentist's' or types of pets at the 'vet's' or storyboards that record children's play and help them recall the experience.

Second, it stimulates play through interactive displays. Such displays allow children to play with, and explore, objects and materials; for example, a table with different kinds of magnets.

The third purpose is related not to the children but to their carers and parents. It is important to communicate to parents the significance of play, to explain how your setting works with their child. An effective way to do this is to have a continually changing display aimed at parents that, through annotated photographs, explains what children are learning through their play. You might take an area such as the sand pit as the theme and show all the things children learn through their sand play. Or you might take an area of learning such as mathematical learning or a disposition such as tenacity and show all the kinds of play through which it develops.

Finally, display can be used by the children as a method of communication. In some settings displays of the available activities (areas) are used to help children make and communicate choices about where they plan to play (for example, High/Scope settings); in others, children mark or put their name cards on activity displays to show where they have played. In this way displays become one of the ways in which children communicate with the adults about their intentions or actions.

Planning provision areas

If play is to provide children with challenging and interesting experiences that help them to learn and to develop, then the provision for play needs to be well planned and resourced. Below (Table 8.1) is an example of how you might plan a resource area. This planning approach requires you to:

- use your own experience and knowledge of children and the early years' curriculum to identify the kinds of activities and learning that might go on in that area
- identify the resources you will need to provide in order to support those activities
- decide how you will manage the area and the resources
- note the key opportunities the area offers for the adult to support the play and the learning

It is important to work from the experiences a child will have, then decide what resources you will make available rather than the other way round. In relation to outdoor play the EYFS (Early Years Foundation Stage) guidance states, 'An approach to outdoor learning that considers experiences rather than equipment places children at the centre of the provision being made' (DfES, 2007: 1).

The first section of the planning pro forma (Table 8.1) outlines permanent resources and set-up; the next shows the enhancement carried out to support the setting's current theme and the final section shows the additional provision in response to a growing interest adults have observed amongst the children.

Table 8.1 Planning for the junk area

Examples of anticipated activities and learning	Resources	Organization	Adult role opportunities
Themed play: Constructing buildings, vehicles and other accessories for children's play. Making pictures, schema-based play especially containing, enveloping and connecting Areas of learning: *Mathematical* – especially comparing and measuring length, using mathematical vocabulary more/less, longer/shorter, heavier/lighter, matching shapes, beginning concepts of volume and area *Knowledge and understanding of the world* – especially investigate using all their senses, ask questions about how things happen and how they work, build and construct with a wide range of resources, select tools and techniques they need to shape, assemble and join materials *Physical* – handle tools and objects safely and with increasing control *Creative* – explore colour, texture, form and space in three dimensions, use imagination in design, express and communicate ideas by designing and making *Communication language and literacy* – interact with others negotiating plans and activities, use talk to sequence and clarify thinking and ideas	Large: Large flat-topped washable table Shelving for storage of materials Small: Tools: scissors, pencils, felt pens, glue spreader, ruler, hole punch Joining materials: masking tape, paper clips, paper fasteners, needles and thread, bull dog clips, PVA glue, sellotape, paper clips, paper fasteners, string, stapler, elastic bands Modelling materials: *Rigid sheets* e.g. thick card, plastic trays, thin hardboard *Flexible sheets* e.g. fabric, paper, cellophane, thin card *Containers* e.g. boxes, egg boxes, paper bags, plastic packaging *Rods* e.g. stems, twigs, sticks, dowelling, pipe cleaners *Tubes* e.g. straws, cardboard tubes, plastic tubing *Threads* e.g. ribbons, rope, wool, raffia, laces	Physical: Sited in a corner of the room next to paint area. Wall-mounted shelves with a shelving unit opposite to form an area with table against the adjacent wall. Modelling materials set out in categories in boxes along shelves. Joining materials and tools in work box on the table. Cleaning materials in a box on a lower shelf. Management: Large storage boxes of materials (by category in store room). Worker identified on a rota to monitor and replenish materials. Children have free access to the area but number of children limited to four.	Key roles: Monitor and ensure safe use of materials. Model use where necessary. Involvement in designing and making. Adult interaction: Scaffolding and sustained shared thinking focused on children's own initiatives will take precedence. Key planned foci for the area from long-term plan. All children: developing language to describe actions and thinking. Younger children: making skills, selecting and deciding. Older children: thinking about characteristics and properties of materials, planning and problem solving.

Table 8.1 (continued)

Examples of anticipated activities and learning	Resources	Organization	Adult role opportunities
Personal, social and emotional – select and use activities and resources independently, work as part of a group, develop positive learning dispositions such as concentration, perseverance and collaboration Skills and competences Cutting, joining, spreading, hand-eye coordination, making patterns, discriminating, evaluating	Units e.g. bottle tops, buttons, plastic ring pulls, fir cones Cleaning-up materials such as brush and shovel		
Provision area enhancement			
Current theme: On the move			
Making transports and resources for journeys Counting, sets, circles Journey narratives Types of transport	Additional material: Selection of wheels Additional strong boxes (for cars/trains etc.) Units suitable for transport furniture and decoration Books/posters with illustrations of cars, boats, trains and aeroplanes	Mary to take the lead on resources and maintenance and will monitor the use of the area	Older children – adults may be needed to model strategies for joining moving wheels and using books for information. Key vocabulary: rotate, circular. All children – encourage planning and problem solving.
Current interests: *Pirates of the Caribbean* (film)			
Children interested in pirate boats, making outfits and treasure chests	Fabric suitable for sails and flags, plasticine, small stones, fixing for lids, poles for flags Book of pirates for pictures of boats, clothing and skull and cross bones etc.	Mary to take the lead on resources and maintenance and will monitor the use of the area: liaise with June who is managing the role-play areas	Opportunities to develop narrative and storying. Talking about symbols.

Activity 8.2: Team meeting

Purpose: To explore strategies for enhancing and evaluating existing play provision.

Again, this is a long activity with several sections so it may need to be done over a period of time.

Decide on an area of provision with which you are least happy, or one you feel is not producing good quality play.

Where you are working as a team you will all need to carry out the following activities between you, therefore you should agree an action plan: who will do what and when? Where the team operates in two or more smaller teams in different rooms then it will help if all teams look at the same kind of provision.

Activity A: Establishing what is in the area

Document the provision, detail what is there already and how the physical provision is set up and managed.

Activity B: Establishing how the area is used

Monitor the use of the area over a period, perhaps a morning and an afternoon session on different days. You should use time sampling (see Table 8.2 for an example) as this will give you the information you need and can be done by someone working nearby without interfering too much with what they are doing, or it can be done by several people who can take turns to observe.

Table 8.2 Provision area monitoring sheet

Area: Junk materials   Date: Time: 1:20 to 3:20   Observers: JD/ML

Time	Who is in the area	What are they doing
0 min	John, Peter, Luke	All looking through the boxes of resources – discussing what they find
5 min	John, Peter, Sam	J&P discussing what they will build. S observing
10 min	John	Looking round the classroom from the area
15 min	Empty	
20 min	Helen, Jane	Looking for something in one of the boxes
30 min	Helen, Jane	Engrossed, trying to fix two boxes together

Activity C: Establishing what learning is going on in the area

Carry out several detailed 10–15-minute observations of individual children working independently in the area; focus on the children's learning and use of the area. Focus especially on the children's levels of involvement, time spent in concentrated play, the kind of learning in which they seem to be involved, levels of cooperation and interaction and how

Activity 8.2 (continued)

children use the resources. Simple diary notes would work well at this point but you might, in addition, think about using photographs.

Activity D: Individual reflection

Where you have worked in a team, all members of staff should have access to copies of all of the observations from Activity B and C in order to reflect on what this tells them about the effectiveness of the provision area.

As individuals, staff should think about how they would enhance the provision area in order to extend the learning opportunities and to increase the children's engagement with the provision. They should make brief notes for themselves of their ideas.

Questions to answer at this point are:

- How much time did children spend in the area?
- What was the range of activities?
- How involved were the children and how sustained was their play?
- What did children seem to be learning and how were they learning?
- Did children of different ages use the provision in the same way?
- Was there evidence that the provision encouraged development/thinking?
- Did you feel that additional or different resources, including space, would have promoted better-quality play?

Further activity

Consider whether there are any other significant findings. If so, how might they assist you in enhancing the area?

Activity 8.3: Enhancing the play opportunities offered by the area

Those working as a team should attempt this activity at a team meeting. Consider what steps you could take to enhance the area. Consider these key aspects:

- where you would site the area
- space allocation
- boundary demarcation
- structural or large equipment (such as a water tray)
- small but permanent resources

- the management and planning of additional resources, for example, things added to coincide with a topic/theme, a curriculum focus or to respond to the needs or current interests of the children

Further activity

At each point think about how this decision might impact on the children and their learning both in terms of what they might learn but also how they might learn. Think about the role the adult must take if the area is to work well.

Activity 8.4: Team meeting

Those working alone should also attempt this activity.

- Draw up an action plan for implementation, monitoring and evaluation of improvements to the area. If you are redesigning areas for children at different developmental stages, consider how they will differ in order to meet curriculum needs or offer more challenge to older/developmentally more advanced children
- Make changes and monitor over an agreed period of time using the methods as above
- At this point also think about how the play might be followed up in small group activities or how it could be used to develop ideas introduced by the practitioner

Activity 8.5: Team meeting

Those working alone should still attempt this activity.

After an agreed period, review progress, make particular note of the areas of learning the children address and the learning disposition they displayed. In the light of your decisions evaluate the provision again. What progress has been made? What difference has it made to the quality of the play?

> ### Activity 8.6: Further activity
>
> Make a large poster, using photographs of the children at play, to communicate to parents what their children are learning by playing in the area. Try to communicate what and how they are learning. This could be attempted at a team meeting.

Summary

This chapter should have raised your awareness of the importance of the physical aspects of the environment to young children's play and learning. It should have supported you in evaluating and developing your own provision. Below is a summary of the key points made in this chapter.

- Well-planned and managed learning environments play an important role in offering children and practitioners effective contexts for learning in all areas of development
- Good physical provision will provide the tools for play, thinking and learning
- Aspects of the physical environment such as the use of space, aesthetics and layout all combine to enhance learning through play
- Continuous provision needs to be carefully planned with a range of rich and varied learning activities in mind, based on the practitioner's experience and knowledge of children but it should remain flexible enough to support children's self-initiated play
- Children should be able to self-manage the resources they need
- Outdoor provision should be as rich and varied as that indoors and where possible should be available at all times
- All provision should take account of children's own concerns and interests
- Resources should be of the best quality the setting can afford and be flexible in their use
- Practitioners should constantly explore strategies for enhancing and evaluating play provision. The key questions to ask are about what the children are learning, how they are learning and how the physical context is supporting that learning

Jargon explained

Ecology of the play context: using this phrase is an attempt to highlight the importance to their play of the relationship between all the aspects of a child's environment.

Provision area: is an area set aside and organized to house one kind of activity – such as water play or construction. It operates as a workshop for the child with all the resources she needs available nearby (see Figures 2.4, 8.2, 8.4).

References

Broadhead, P. (2003), *Early Years Play and Learning: Developing Social Skills and Cooperation*. London: Routledge Falmer.

DfES (2007), Effective Practice: Outdoor Learning (CD ROM), in *Early Years Foundation Stage: Setting the Standards for Learning, Development and Care for Children from Birth to Five*. London: DfES.

Siraj-Blatchford, I., Sylva, K., Muttock, S., Gilden, R. and Bell, D. (2002), *Researching Effective Pedagogy in the Early Years*. DfES.

The Role of the Adult in Supporting Sustained Meaningful Play: Intervention

Chapter Outline

Introduction	154
What do we mean by intervention?	156
Why intervene?	157
What intervention strategies do settings adopt?	157
How can we intervene successfully?	159
What approaches might we adopt?	161
When might we choose not to intervene?	174
Jargon explained, Further reading, References	176

Introduction

The adult's role in providing an appropriate physical and intellectual environment that meets the child's needs is crucial to the learning process. An essential element of the learning environment for young children will be well-supported, good quality play; to achieve this, practitioners need to intervene skilfully in play.

Purpose of this chapter

This chapter continues to develop the framework for observation and will consider how adults can support sustained and meaningful learning in both adult-initiated and child-initiated play. This will include how adults can work with groups and individuals in play situations using strategies such as resource-based intervention and oral strategies such as questioning, storying and sustained shared thinking. It will support the reader in developing skilled intervention that facilitates learning, by helping them to make judgements about how they might best scaffold children's thinking.

The chapter will help you to:

- understand the role of the adult in supporting and sustaining meaningful play
- understand what intervention is
- consider your setting's overall strategy
- understand the many forms of intervention
- consider a set of key principles that should guide intervention
- develop your intervention skills

Figure 9.1 Intervention is all the things we do as adults to support and extend children's play and learning

---

Activity 9.1: Personal learning journal

Purpose: To identify your present understanding of the role of the adult in play.

As an individual, consider what you think are the roles of adults in children's play. We suggest that you begin with 'My role in children's play is to…' and then bullet-point your ideas using only key words. Record these notes in the first section of a personal learning journal sheet. Now reflect on what you have written and consider why you think as you do. Note down the key influences on your ideas, for example, 'It is what I have seen others do.' Keep these notes as you will return to them at the end of the chapter.

Further activity

Try to order the roles you have identified in their order of significance beginning with the most important item.

What do we mean by intervention?

The use of the phrase 'intervention' indicates that interaction, especially verbal communication, is not the only strategy for extending and supporting children's learning; it suggests a much more sensitive and responsive role for the adult and is the opposite of interference, interrogation and interruption. Intervention is all the things we as adults do to support and extend children's play and learning. The term intervention implies a more complex role for the adult as supporter, facilitator, enabler, negotiator, informant and instructor.

The concept of scaffolding

The principal purpose of intervention is to support children in their play and to scaffold their learning. You will remember from Chapter 2 that scaffolding refers to a 'process that enables a child or novice to solve a problem, carry out a task, or achieve a goal that would be beyond his unassisted efforts' (Wood, Bruner and Ross 1976). It is about all you do to assist children to achieve a higher level of thinking than they would if working alone. Through skilful scaffolding adults challenge and extend children's current level of development; beginning where the learner is, they draw on existing skills and knowledge but provide support so that the child is able to move through her zone of proximal development (ZPD) (see Chapter 2).

Scaffolding children's learning can operate at very different levels of intensity. There is a continuum of scaffolding from simple actions that will allow children to make sense of an activity, such as modelling how to open a box, to Socratic questioning techniques that help them make sense of complex ideas. The continuum also includes direct interventions during play such as focused teaching and 'sustained shared thinking' and indirect interventions such as providing opportunities for peer interaction and setting up play environments into which are embedded learning opportunities. This chapter is about how we can scaffold children's learning.

Why intervene?

Through direct teaching children can learn facts about the world which they need simply to remember, but 'concepts', which are concerned with ideas and principles, need to be constructed by the child. The role of others is to help the children in their construction of knowledge and understanding. As you read in Chapter 2, although children actively construct their own learning they do so in the context of their world and with the assistance of other, more knowledgeable individuals. Intervention in its many forms provides a rich context that supports learning.

What intervention strategies do settings adopt?

There is a continuum of interventional strategies adopted within early years settings grouped around five basic approaches.

Non-intervening

In this approach adults provide a rich environment and supervise the setting in order to ensure the children's safety – they do not intervene in the children's activities.

Prescribing

In this approach adults tell the children what they are to do either by setting tasks or by providing equipment that can only be used in ways determined by the adult.

Re-directing

In this approach adults allow children to initiate their own activity and are actively involved with the children. However, the adult tends to steer the child in a direction that reflects their own thinking and concerns rather than those of the children.

Extending

This approach also involves the provision of a good range and quality of resources with children initiating their own activities, but it differs from re-directing significantly. In this approach adults observe what children are doing to determine the focus of attention; they find out what the child is thinking about, what the child is interested in. This guides the adult's intervention; strategies are adopted that elaborate and extend the activity, and the learning that it supports.

Collaborating

Whilst providing all that the extending approach offers, this approach differs in the relationship of the child and the adult; it sees play as a collaborative endeavour. The adult and the child play together; they develop a shared understanding, a shared dialogue and play script; they make meaning as a joint venture although the control of the play remains in the hands of the child.

Although the overriding approach adopted by modern early years settings now falls clearly within the 'extending' category of approaches and some settings are adopting more collaborative learning, there are occasions when any setting might adopt any one of the other strategies.

For example, on one occasion in a nursery that normally adopts an 'extending' approach a prescribing approach was adopted when woodwork tools were to be introduced to the setting for the first time. In preparation for the introduction, and to ensure the safe use of the tools in independent activities, a closely supervised activity was set up during independent activity time. All children were encouraged to take part and were taught how to use the tools safely and, under supervision, practised using the tools. On another occasion children were left to play in the construction area without any intervention for a long period because the play was progressing well with good internal support from the more-experienced children (a non-intervening approach).

Activity 9.2: Personal learning journal

Purpose: To consider the approach adopted in your setting.

Look at your diary of a day that you completed as part of the 'Personal development: Reviewing current knowledge and understanding' section, in Chapter 6. Using one colour for each of the approaches outlined above, mark each of your activities according to where they sit on the continuum of interventional strategies. What is the balance of approaches you adopted?

Further activity

Look carefully at your results and consider whether the balance is related to the kind of play with which you are involved.

Team meeting

Share these results with your team and try to assess the overall pattern for the setting.

Further activity

Again, look at the balance of approaches and consider how the type of play across the setting influences the approaches the adults use.

How can we intervene successfully?

Where the relationship the adult has with the child is a controlling and directing one, the child is deprived of autonomy and becomes unable or unwilling to act and to think independently; his confidence and initiative are eroded. Whilst directing children to do things appears to work in the short term, the lack of 'flow of thought' that results from intrinsic/self-motivation, promoted by self-initiated or self-managed activity, leaves the child unable to extend or develop the activity without further instructions. There develops what has become known as a 'cycle of dependency'. Adult intervention that takes account of, and is directed by, the child's own concerns and needs, engages the powerful potential of the child's innate desire to make sense of the world.

When practitioners intervene in play they need to do so sensitively. They need to be aware of what the child is trying to achieve and what the child's concerns are. This allows them to identify the best ways in which to support the child without taking over, leading the play and preventing the child from retaining a sense of autonomy. The work you did about children's views of play (Activity 6.4 in Chapter 6) is relevant here.

Activity 9.3: Personal learning journal

Purpose: To highlight and increase your skills as a play partner.

As an individual, observe a child for long enough to find out what they are trying to achieve through their play. Now join in the play as a partner. If you have difficulty thinking about what this would 'look' like, imagine how another child would join in. Try to sustain this for five minutes. Remain the junior partner; do not try to lead or extend the play; listen carefully to what the child says; watch what they do; take your lead from them and keep the balance of talk equal or in the child's favour.

Using a personal learning journal record sheet, record factual information about the event in the first section. Now in the second section reflect on what you learned about the child's intentions and concerns, and what you learned about their knowledge and understanding. Note down the key points and consider what you have learned and what questions the incident raises for you.

Team meeting

Share your notes with the rest of the team. Together think of ways in which you could have extended the child's learning along lines that reflect the child's concerns. After the meeting use this information to complete the third section of your sheet.

Further activity

Complete the fourth section of the personal learning journal record sheet, by reflecting on your own success in analysing and communicating your ideas to others. For example, could you identify what you had learned clearly?

If you are working alone you should still do the individual elements of this activity.

Key principles of intervention

If intervention is to meet the needs of the child then the adult must:

- first consider what is actually happening inside the child's head whilst they play – what is the child doing; what does observation tell you about what is of value and interest to the child?
- plan interventions based upon your knowledge of the child, the knowledge gained from the observation about what the child is currently playing at, and how this might lead on to new learning
- consider what interventional strategies will best scaffold the learning
- keep within the child's ZPD, that is, provide challenge without frustration and failure
- engage in the play in such a way that its continuance does not depend on your presence
- remain flexible, constantly review the situation and tailor your action to the child's response

What approaches might we adopt?

From a consideration of the nature of scaffolding it becomes clear that there are many ways to support children's learning. Although we will now look at approaches in discrete categories, different approaches might be used simultaneously.

Resource-based intervention

This is the introduction of new resources to support play development, and is the least complex approach. It requires the adult to identify opportunities to extend learning by the addition or the removal of resources guided by her observation of play and her knowledge of the child's developmental level.

For example, in one setting a group were constructing a den in the outdoor area; the adult noticed that they were struggling with ways to make a roof and that there were no appropriate materials for this purpose available to them. As the group were supporting each other's thinking and there were high levels of collaboration, she decided simply to take a collection of fabric sheets outside, put them on the ground near to the group and say, 'I thought these might help'.

In another setting two children were using small containers to fill up two bottles, counting as they put each container of water into the bottles and comparing how many containers of water were used in each bottle. The adult noticed that they were becoming frustrated as they were having difficulty scooping water up because a younger child, who had just left the water tray, had emptied all the resources from the shelves in the water area, into the trough. The practitioner went over and removed all the things the children were not using and replaced them on the shelves. On another occasion she might have asked them to solve the problem of access to the water or to help her remove the resources but in this instance she decided not to intervene further as they were very engrossed in their play. Further observation revealed that her action allowed the children to move on and to identify that escaping water was a problem; they now noticed the funnel that had been replaced on the shelf and decided to try that.

There are occasions when the addition of new resources will require some additional support from the adult, perhaps to model their use or to help integrate them into their play.

For example, a more mature child is constructing a model of a robot with cardboard boxes. She has available a range of fastenings that provide for fixed positions but from the observation it becomes obvious that she is thinking about how she might make the arms of the robot move. One approach might be simply to offer her brass paper-fasteners, commenting 'These might help you'. However, it may be more appropriate to model their use at this point, as effective and safe use requires particular techniques.

One practitioner observing role play noticed that the children were involved in 'getting the shopping in'; the 'parent' was giving instructions to the 'child' about what had to be bought.

Drawing on 'Don't Forget the Bacon' (Hutchins 2002)which they had been reading with one of the practitioners, they were discussing the need to remember what was required. The practitioner recalled that both children had been involved with emergent writing and so decided to introduce the idea of a shopping list. She went into the play in role as the next door neighbour and engaged the children in a conversation that explored how the 'child' was going to remember all the shopping. One child suggested that they could write it down; at this point the 'neighbour' offered them the use of her shopping list pad and showed them how she used it. She then left the play saying she had to go and cook the dinner. She continued to observe, noting the children's concentrated attempts to invent symbols for each item.

Figure 9.2 Additional resources have been provided by the adult to support children as they represent their play symbolically

Experiential-based intervention

One strategy that can be used to support learning is to provide an experience from which children can then draw to enrich their play and so extend their learning. A common example of this is where practitioners arrange for a visit to a local supermarket to enrich the play where a shop has been set up. Another successful approach is to invite someone to visit the setting, for example, many settings host visits from the fire service. Although they can be used to stimulate interest, these visits are most successful where they result from children's own interests and play themes. There are also smaller-scale internally provided experiences that are used in a similar way, such as building a snowman, bubble making, inviting older children in to perform a play. What all these things have in common is that they are not part of the continuous provision; they are rich, multi-sensory experiences in which children can become completely involved and to which they can respond in a number of ways. The experience itself is of value but it also enriches the children's play afterwards.

Example: A group of boys had been playing robbers; their play was very physical, focused on running backwards and forwards, jumping on each other and shouting 'I've got you! You can't get away' and getting the response 'No you haven't 'cos I can fight you.' The practitioner decided that the play was of poor quality, was not developing and was in danger of spilling over into inappropriate behaviour. She decided to invite the local policeman into the nursery to talk to all the children about his job. He showed them his police equipment and talked about all the things he did during the day; his radio, handcuffs and notebook were of particular interest to the 'robbers' group. After he left, the practitioner planned to observe and intervene in the 'robbers'' play. As she had anticipated, the visit stimulated much better quality play; she provided a range of new resources and intervened to support the new scenario.

Modelling play

For very young children or those children who find it difficult to play, perhaps because they have little experience of it, modelling play can be a very effective strategy. Again there will be a continuum, from playing in parallel beside the child but not communicating, to becoming involved as a play partner, to direct teaching. Playing in parallel may work best where children withdraw from others or avoid direct communication such as in the case of very shy children or those wary of adults. Becoming a play partner may help where children's play fails to develop or where they are having difficulty playing cooperatively. It can also be used to help children whose gendered play is restricting their learning opportunities. Teaching children games, especially traditional outdoor games, is an example of the most direct form of modelling.

Interactive intervention

This is the most demanding of the intervention strategies for most practitioners as it requires the adult to be responsive to what the child is doing and saying on an extended ongoing basis.

The 'Researching Effective Pedagogy in the Early Years' project (Siraj-Blatchford et al. 2002) found that:

- in successful settings cognitive interactions were more frequent, involved shared thinking between adults and children and were most effective when initiated by children and sustained by teachers

- in pre-school settings that the researchers described as 'excellent' they found that interactions between adults and children were very high; for example, adults encouraged children to try new experiences, asked questions that provoked speculation and looked for opportunities to support their learning and extend their imaginations
- in 'excellent' pre-school settings teacher-directed learning was combined with children's play and a stimulating environment; around half of the interactions were child initiated compared with about 15% in 'good' settings (GTC 2003)

Although children will learn through playing alone they make better progress where adults involve themselves directly in the play. Through skilful intervention adults enrich the learning experience and enhance the child's learning through a co-construction of learning. Such intervention, which involves sustained shared and explicit thinking, whilst allowing the child to retain responsibility and control over the learning, supports and encourages the child to reflect and to extend and deepen her learning. Later in the chapter we will look in more detail at this strategy.

Interaction is not just about talking. When we interact with children there is a temptation to think only of talking with them; however, although verbal interaction is the basis for much communication and learning, a range of modes for expressing, interpreting and sharing ideas and understanding needs to be made available. You will remember from your reading of Chapter 2 that meaning is not 'extracted' from the messages that others send us or the things we experience but constructed by our brains using the information we receive and knowledge we have already in order to make it 'make sense' to us. Therefore, in understanding something, a rich variety of communication modes will give children more information in different forms which can be used to construct more accurate models of the world. For all children multi-sensory communication is important.

Activity 9.4: Personal learning journal

Purpose: To identify what forms of communication are used by children and adults in your setting.

Communicating is about gaining and sharing information and understanding. Think about what forms of communication adults and children use in your own setting; you might go back to the observations you have done in previous activities or note down what you observe whilst you are working. The categories are very diverse but might include language, touch, image making, modelling, music, movement, rhythm, smell, tasting and exploring with the mouth.

Keep these notes for the next team meeting.

What do we mean by good quality interaction?

Interaction indicates a two-way process in which all participants play an active role; it involves two-way communication. Although conversation is a verbal interaction, mirroring a young child's actions is a physical interaction, drawing images together a visual interaction; many interventions combine several forms of interaction. Good quality interaction involves the players in communicating and sharing thoughts and ideas in a meaningful way. It is as important for the child's learning to express his own ideas, to ask questions, to focus on what he is interested in, as it is to learn about the ideas of others and answer questions.

You will recall that writers such as Vygotsky and Bruner (Chapter 2) pointed out that social interaction between the child and other, more experienced individuals within the child's culture was an essential component of learning and recent research has associated improved thinking skills with the quality of adult–child interaction (see Sylva et al. 2004).

Strategies for interaction

The strategies you adopt will be determined by the knowledge you bring of the child to the interaction and the purpose of your intervention, but there are key guiding principles.

Principles of interaction in play in the early years setting

Preparing to interact

Maximize your chances of developing a meaningful and effective interaction by tuning in to the child – stop, observe, reflect and then engage:

- Hold back before taking action
- Observe the actions of the child and consider what feelings and thoughts they might indicate
- Reflect on the child's meaning or intentions in what he does. What is the child concerned with?
- Think about what you already know about the child. What interests the child? You need to tune in to children's concerns, their 'internal curriculum' and link this with your knowledge of curriculum and of how children learn. (Think here about what you have read in Chapter 1 about observation.)
- Position yourself alongside the child: adopt a relaxed position, ideally one in which you are at the child's level and can make eye contact
- Know why you are joining in with an activity. What are your intentions?
- Interact in all activities equally. Be aware of your own activity preferences that are perhaps a result of the value you put on activities or the ease with which you can join in. For example, it is common to find that practitioners find it easier to become involved in play with mark making and paint rather than construction play. Any such bias needs to be monitored

Supporting the child's thinking

Interactions need to be supportive, therefore:

- accept the child's initiatives
- encourage the child to keep control of the interaction
- allow enough time for a quality interaction to develop
- let the child see that you are enjoying the experience
- make fewer interactions, but for longer periods. This develops the best quality learning; however, you should take your timing from the child – young children especially may only want or be able to engage in short anecdotal exchanges
- be aware of what the next steps in the child's learning might be
- be aware of those children who do not engage adults

Extending the child's learning

- Stay alert to the possibilities of extension but use this thoughtfully; think about challenging the child's thinking at a level he can deal with
- Think about all the ways we communicate; allow and encourage different ways of communicating; talk is not the only way
- Encourage the child to think more deeply through reflecting, solving problems, imagining, explaining, representing, exploring and so on
- Reflecting on when and how you interact
- Monitor not only how much time you give to different groups of children, such as girls and boys and younger and older children, but also what the nature of the interaction is. For example, do you talk about different things; do they take different roles in conversation? All these things will influence the learning opportunities for different groups of children.
- Consider whether your interaction improved the children's play and learning.
- Join in and leave activities sensitively; avoid your role becoming essential to the play so that it ceases when you withdraw.

The functions interaction plays can be crucial to a child's learning:

- *Transfer of learning*: Interaction can help children decide upon the most appropriate problem-solving strategy for the task in hand. By helping to make the links between different learning experiences explicit, common features can be identified in order for children to transfer learning from one aspect to another. The adult can do this by reminding children of what they have done previously, pointing out similarities and differences, highlighting skills and knowledge the child may have already that could be used to solve a problem
- *Promoting children's involvement in learning*: Interacting with children in small groups increases their

involvement; they are less likely to be passive observers and the adults are more likely to have authentic conversations with them. The adult can do this by, for example, going into the role play in role

- *Facilitating children's cognitive and linguistic development*: The most powerful tool for learning is language; children need language with which to develop their thinking (Chapter 2). The adult can facilitate learning by providing the vocabulary associated with activities. There is a range of strategies for doing this, including providing a commentary on the play ('You've made the wheel spin'), telling the child the word for something they are talking to you about ('This shape has a special name; it's called a triangle'), and sharing your own thinking ('I think the tower needs to be more stable')
- *Discussing processes within activities*: This supports children in making sense of transformations. The adult can do this by talking with the child about such things as cause and effect, and starting and end points ('I wonder why the wheel went faster when you used the big jug to pour the water?')
- *Focusing children's attention on significant aspects of what they are doing*: In line with our understanding of brain development and the social context of learning we should help children see connections and observe changes brought about by the actions they are performing. ('Oh look, where your red stripe and blue stripe overlap it's turned purple')
- *Developing metacognition*: Interaction can help children to become aware of how they are learning; this also includes helping children to develop and then remember memorizing strategies. The adult may do this by working alongside the child and providing a commentary on what they are doing, commenting on an action, talking to them about the strategies they have used to complete an activity. In this way they also provide the children with the language they need to think about their thinking. ('This is a bit of a problem isn't it; can you remember what you did when it got stuck yesterday?')

Talking with children

The principles of good educational conversation are:

- the child initiates the conversation (this may be non-verbal)
- the conversation is a shared experience; the adults are talk partners
- the adult listens as well as talks: active listening involves non-verbal signals and concentration on what the other person is saying
- the conversation is sustained rather than brief; the length of the conversation will be determined by the interest, maturity and ability of the child
- the conversation is authentic; it follows the rules of normal adult conversation and will involve a range of thinking skills and knowledge
- it allows children the opportunity to explore ideas that challenge or intrigue them
- the adult takes account of the child's home language patterns

Encouraging narrative

Young children relate their experiences in the form of stories, and so formulating a story becomes a powerful way of making sense of their experience. It is through stories that children are able to speculate and hypothesize about possible consequences of events and predict possible outcomes. The experience of 'telling stories', or building narratives, as a young child has a significant influence on the child's ability to write effectively at a later stage. Several forms of play are particularly valuable in allowing children to 'story'; these include role play, small world play and construction play. In order to encourage children to develop narrative or recount, we must adopt strategies that are not merely lists of questions to which children know we know the answer. We need to listen carefully and ask questions that take the child further in her thinking, that explore her concerns and which allow her to find ways of first expressing her thoughts, then re-thinking, reassessing and then articulating the new thinking.

Questioning

Questioning is not a true strategy but a tool that could be used as part of a strategy. Skilful questioning is an invaluable skill for the practitioner. There are many studies of adults' use of questions with children but all suggest that in schools and other settings there is an over reliance on low-level closed questioning and little use of more challenging open questions related to children's learning that get children to think and to reason. A recent study found that in pre-school settings over 60% of questions were found to be unrelated to children's learning (Siraj-Blatchford et al. 2002) and observation in settings reveals that much of this questioning is social or managerial in nature. The conversation with a three-year-old, below, shows the potential quite simple question forms have for extending children's thinking during play.

Case Study 9.1

Child: (playing with play dough and baking tools) I'm making cakes.

Adult: Oh, what kind of cakes are they?

Child: Real cakes.

Adult: Does that mean I can really eat them?

Child: No silly, because they are pretend real cakes.

Adult: That means I can pretend to eat them.

Child: I can make real cakes to really eat.

Adult: Will they be different from these ones?

Child: You have to make them with things that your mummy gets from Tesco's.

Adult: What things do you have to get from the shop then?

Case Study 9.1 (continued)

Child: Eggs and sugar…and then you do mixing and then you put them in the oven but you have to be careful because it can burn you. I'm going to put these cakes in the oven now to get done.

Here the adult gets an answer to her first question that she is not expecting; she follows the child's focus and explores the idea of what 'real' implies. She encourages the child to compare, to recall, to make judgements, to make decisions but the child retains control of the interaction.

Case Study 9.2

A group of children are in the construction area; they seem to want to build high structures but with little success.

Child 1: (to adult) We made a really big one but it crashed.

Adult: How big was it?

Child 2: As big as six.

Child 1: (counting indicating points in the air beginning at the floor) 1, 2, 3, 4, 5, 6, as big as six.

Adult: So what are you trying to do?

Child 1: Build a really big one 1, 2, 3, 4, 5, 6, 7, 10, 100 (again using hand gestures to indicate a growing structure).

Adult: So why do you think it keeps crashing? Why does it fall down?

Child 2: Because it's too big high and it just falls.

Adult: Do you want to try again?

Child 1: To as big as the ceiling?

Adult: We could try.

(The adult acts as builder's mate, passing bricks as they play. The tower begins to wobble.)

Adult: What's happening to the tower?

Child 2: It's going to fall so it wobbles.

> **Case Study 9.2 (continued)**
>
> Adult: (to Child 1) What do you think?
>
> Child 1: Yes. It just wobbles and it wobbles over.
>
> Adult: I wonder whether we can stop it wobbling.
>
> The temptation for the practitioner here is to latch on to the counting, and in some circumstances this would be a good judgement, but in this case the children's play is focused on building a high tower so she follows this through. It offers her the opportunity to extend the children's thinking by highlighting significant events and supporting them in making connections of cause and effect. Later in the interaction she introduces them to the concept of stable and steady.

Sustained shared thinking

> We found that the 'excellent' settings encouraged relatively more 'sustained shared thinking'. By this we mean an episode in which two or more individuals 'work together' in an intellectual way to solve a problem, clarify a concept, evaluate activities, extend a narrative etc. Both parties must contribute to the thinking and it must develop and extend thinking…Our investigations of adult–child interaction lead us to believe that periods of 'sustained shared thinking' are a necessary prerequisite for excellent early years practice, especially where this is also encouraged in the home through parent support (Sylva et al. 2004: 36).

An overarching term adopted for describing adult–child interactions in which both child and adult are involved as active partners and where the adult uses the interaction to extend or enrich the child's learning is 'sustained shared thinking'; Bruner's term for this was 'joint involvement episodes'. Such periods of interaction have been shown to be particularly valuable in terms of children's learning. The EPPE project indicated that in excellent settings such interactions were more frequent than in other settings, that they were more likely to occur in one-to-one interactions and that child-initiated play provided the best opportunity for such interactions. This is not surprising given what we know about how children learn (Chapter 2) because such episodes offer the opportunity for the co-construction of learning by allowing the child and the adult to construct an idea or activity together and to draw from the child's experience of the world. They allow the adult to offer cognitive challenge beyond what the child could do unaided by providing structured support, in other words, scaffolding.

This approach to interaction can and will draw on the skilled use of questions, especially open questions such as 'What do you think might happen if…?' However, in becoming a 'thinking partner' the adult will need to establish the same ethos of equality as they would with another adult through such things as communicating genuine interest and respecting the other person's ideas and choices. They will need to be able to recognize the child's concerns, be sensitive and responsive to what the child says and does and recognize what is within the child's ZPD. The adult will draw on the same range of strategies they might use in conversations with other adults such as inviting the child to elaborate (and then what happened…), offering their own experience (I have a cat at home that…), suggesting (I think that…), offering prompts to remind (when you did this you said that…), encouraging the child by pointing out their achievements so far (you have thought that through really well; now we need to think about…), offering alternative points of view (perhaps the fireman would be too scared to…) and modelling thinking aloud (I thought that…but then I looked at…and remembered…). However, these strategies will only be effective where the adult has developed an open and trusting relationship with the child so that they accept the adult as a partner who is genuinely interested in what they do and what they think.

When is the best time to intervene in play?

As Rogoff (1990) explains, using a Vygotskian approach to interaction maintains the child's motivation, feelings of mastery and sense of agency. Essential to this approach is the judgements the practitioner makes about when to intervene and when to withdraw and leave the child to work alone. It is a judgement informed by the concept of the 'zone of proximal development' and the practitioner's understanding of what will challenge a child at the limits of her skills and knowledge.

If you follow the principles this book sets out and adopt observation as one of your ongoing key roles then you will begin to recognize opportunities throughout the sessions, in what they do and say, for extending children's play. You will begin to recognize situations where adult intervention will take children's learning on and those occasions when it may not. There are also times during intervention when you recognize that the child needs a period of consolidation, of playing by themselves or with other children when you will withdraw.

Case Study 9.3

A four-year-old was observed in the water trough. She began the session using a funnel to fill a wide see-through tube with water. Her attempt fails because she does not hold both ends up to prevent the water escaping as she fills the tube. The adult approaches her.

A: You seem to have a problem, Beth.

B: Yes, it's not working.

A: What are you trying to do?

B: I want to fill the tube so I can splash the water outside but the water keeps escaping.

A: I wonder why it's escaping.

B: I think it's because it keeps running out of the bottom.

A: Ah it's running down the tube out of the bottom.

B: Yes, see.

(The child continues to pour; the adult holds the tube up at the other end a little.)

B: It's stopped.

(The child continues to fill and the water begins to overflow again.)

B: Oh no it's happening again. Can you hold it up more higher and make more room for the water at your end?

Although Beth did not seem to understand about water levels she is beginning to recognize that if you alter the height of the tube at the other end the water stays in the tube. At this point the adult holds the tube up, the child fills it and then carries it by both ends to the outside area where, holding one end, she spins round and splashes the water onto the hot flagstones. At this point the practitioner leaves Beth to play on her own.

Observation of Beth later in the session reveals that she continues to fill the tube and works out that the game works best if she keeps up both ends of the tube at the same level; she recruits the help of another child to achieve this.

In discussion with the other practitioner at the end of the day, she discovers that several children's play in the water has involved water levels; they play at how far they can tip the containers before the water flows out – one child made the comment that the water is flat. The practitioners plan to colour the water dark blue the next day to draw the children's attention to the water levels; they add several see-through containers to the water area and note down key vocabulary they might introduce.

There are particular times when you will plan to intervene because of the child or the event. For example, children with poor concentration often lack organizational ability (see Chapter 3) in relation to materials, tasks, order of action, visualizing the end product. They need help with the process, not so much the end product; they need support in planning, choosing resources, deciding on the sequence of events. You may plan to intervene with these children on a regular basis.

Other examples of why adults pre-plan to get involved with play:

- To help children recall the memory of a visit, through play, books or movement, which helps them reactivate the memory – to make sense and embed learning
- Following an activity through
- Attracting children to particular activities, for example, girls to the construction play. Where the adult becomes involved with an activity, the status of that activity is raised in the eyes of the children; this is particularly true of same-sex children
- Where staff have identified low-level, stereotypical play. Such play can be reduced when staff become involved and challenge stereotyping and prejudice

Intervention strategies for ensuring appropriate behaviour

Inappropriate behaviour during play can present an enormous problem in some settings; it distresses other children, takes up enormous amounts of practitioners' time and interferes with the miscreant's own learning. However, there are key interventions that will ameliorate this problem:

- Providing quality provision – poor quality play materials are frustrating and unreliable
- Providing a sufficient quantity of resources – insufficient resources not only cause aggression and impatience in children because they do not have access to materials but also prevent groups of children from working on collaborative play and building their social skills
- Ensuring children's interests are captured by providing a play space planned around their interests and needs. Children who spend time in a context that they do not find stimulating and which does not challenge them and engage their interest are unlikely to become involved and sustain concentration

The physical environment affects the behaviour and emotional response of children and adults alike. Time and thought needs to be given to the design of the physical environment, to ensure children's sense of well-being and to maximize their ability to cope successfully with the challenges it offers. Practitioners need to concern themselves about all aspects of the environment from the aesthetic of the setting, such as colour and vista on the one hand, to more practical issues such as the proximity of washing facilities to the paint table on the other (see Chapter 8).

Learning to deal with conflict is like any other learning: children need to practise with support, to have the process modelled for them, to feel safe to make mistakes sometimes but most of all to think it through. They need to develop an understanding so that they can operate independently in varied situations. Intervening to ensure diffusion of conflict or inappropriate behaviour in play can be dealt with using any of the five interventional strategies discussed above: non-intervening, prescribing, re-directing, extending and collaborating. Again, there may be situations when any of the five approaches may be appropriate. For example, a practitioner may judge that a low-level disagreement is best left for the children to resolve and so will monitor the situation but not intervene; on the other hand, where children's safety is compromised the adult might take a prescribing approach initially. However, for long-term gains in social and emotional development a 'problem-solving approach to conflict' works best. In this situation the adult scaffolds the children's conflict resolution; sustained shared thinking is particularly appropriate in this situation.

When might we choose not to intervene?

Where children have control of their play they are good at including or excluding adults when they want to. The skilled practitioner will be sensitive to this and take it into account when deciding to intervene. Research, and the experience of practitioners on the ground, shows that where adults become involved in children's play there is an increase in the quality of the play and the learning gains for the children. There will be times, however, when it is better to step back and let children work alone or with their peers, for example:

- When the child is engrossed in her own play and your observation suggests that she is working in a focused and purposeful way.
- When the child is working well with others, the play is of good quality and the interaction indicates that children's thinking and learning is moving on. Remember children can learn from each other and adults are not always necessary. Even quite young children work well together and this has been shown to improve quality and the intellectual challenge of their play.
- When the resources the child has at her disposal are supporting her well at this point in her learning. Where the child is learning about the materials she is using for herself and she is formulating her own theories, the adult needs to let her have enough time to develop ideas.

Even where adults have initiated a play activity they may, once it is under way, allow the child time to develop the play before intervening further.

At a practical level, it is important that your setting plans and supports independent play as this allows practitioners to spend more sustained periods of time supporting learning rather than moving quickly from one activity to another.

Activity 9.5: Personal learning journal

Purpose: To develop your skills and understanding of good quality scaffolding.

Ideally you will need access to a video camera for this activity but use can be made of an audio tape recorder.

Video- or tape-record your interactions with a child or children during their play, first working in the way you normally work, then allowing the children to lead the conversation, and finally work with a child keeping in mind the principles of intervention explored earlier in the chapter.

Fill in the first section of the personal learning journal record sheet, noting the three contexts. In the second section note down the differences you noticed in the interactions, for example, the balance of adult–child talk, whose interests were followed, the children's confidence and willingness to take initiatives, how well ideas were developed.

Complete the second section of the form noting what you have learned from the analysis, the third section noting what you would do differently next time you intervene in play and finally the fourth section where you should identify what you think are your strengths and weaknesses and what you need to learn or find out about in order to become more effective.

Further activity

In addition, analyse the recordings, noting the forms of communication used and the impact.

Activity 9.6: Team meeting

All practitioners should come to the meeting prepared to identify what they feel are the strengths and weaknesses of their scaffolding skills. In discussion with the team, individuals should set themselves targets for working on the most significant areas they have identified as a weakness. Common targets should be identified and, as a team, decisions should be made about what support can be given. For example, one practitioner who has strength in an area may be willing to talk about what she does or may be willing to be observed by her colleagues.

Activity 9.6 (continued)

Further activity

One effective way of making progress with scaffolding skills is to ask colleagues to observe each other, focusing on agreed areas. We suggest that staff work in self-chosen pairs, observing each other and using an agreed checklist of 'good practice'. This should be generated by the team using the information in this chapter and what they learned from the previous activity.

The observations should then be discussed between partners and new targets set.

Remember to record what happens in your personal learning journal.

Activity 9.7: Personal learning journal

Purpose: To review personal learning.

Revisit your personal learning journal record sheet to review what you thought about the roles of adults in children's play and what influenced your ideas (earlier in this chapter).

- How have your views changed? Note any key changes in the second section of the sheet
- In the next section note any changes or planned changes in your practice
- In the final section consider what you think the barriers to change might be and how they might be overcome

Further activity

Throughout the activity also consider the order of importance you assigned to the roles.

Jargon explained

Emergent writing: early forms of mark making intended by the child to represent 'writing'.

Play script: an agreed, outline, form and progress of play.

Types of questions

Closed: These are questions such as 'What is your name?', 'Do you like playing in the sand?', that require only a short, non-elaborated answer.

Open: These are questions such as 'What do you think might happen next?', 'How might we make this tower more stable?', that ask for a more elaborated answer and encourage a more thoughtful response.

Socratic questioning: A good way to help children think about something is to ask them a question about it; good questions help them put information they already know together, examine their current understandings and create new ideas. Socratic questions involve observing (listening and watching) the learner carefully in order to judge and phrase your question in a way that will help her think. Socratic questions are specifically intended to help others learn rather than test them. There are different categories of questions, for example, those that seek clarification ('Can you explain that…?', 'What do you mean by…?'), probe reasons and assumptions ('Why do you think that?', 'How do you know that?'), explore alternative views ('Do you think other people would agree with that?', 'What do you think… would think?'), test implications and consequences ('What would happen if you did that?', 'How could we find out if that was true?') and ask about the question/problem ('How will your idea help?', 'Have we solved the problem?').

Further reading

Reggio Emilia

If you are interested in different approaches to representation in pre-school, the pre-schools in Reggio Emilia (Italy) have an approach to the education of children that values a great number of ways of re-presenting experience. Children are given opportunities for expressing their ideas and their feelings in many graphic and non-graphic forms, both as individuals and as members of a group. Adults work alongside children supporting and instructing; they observe what the children do and say and then plan further experiences with the children's preoccupations in mind. There are many interesting books about Reggio including:

The Reggio Emilia Approach to Early Years Education (1999, revised edition 2006). This is a good introduction to Reggio, which you can obtain through Customer Services at Learning and Teaching Scotland.
Thornton, L. and Brunton, P. (2005), *Understanding the Reggio Approach*. David Fulton.
Abbott, L. and Nutbrown, C. (eds) (2001), *Experiencing Reggio Emilia: Implications for Pre-school Provision*. Open University Press.

References

GTC (2003), *Researching Effective Pedagogy in the Early Years Summary*. Available at http://www.gtce.org.uk/research/romtopics/rom_curriculum/early_years_jan03 (accessed September 2007).

Hutchins, P. (2002), *Don't Forget the Bacon*. LOndon: Red Fox.

Rogoff, B. (1990), *Apprenticeship in Thinking: Cognitive Development in Social Context*. Oxford University Press.

Siraj-Blatchford, I., Sylva, K., Matlock, S., Gilden, R. and Bell, D. (2002), *Researching Effective Pedagogy in the Early Years*. DfES.

Sylva, K., Helhuish, E., Sammons, P., Siraj-Blatchford, I. and Taggart, Brenda (2004), *The Effective Provision of Pre-School Education (EPPE) Project: Final Report*. DfES.

Wood, D., Bruner, J.S. and Ross, G. (1976), 'The Role of Tutoring in Problem Solving'. *Journal of Child Psychology and Psychiatry* 17, 89–100.

Planning: Developing a Framework for Children's Learning Through Play

10

Chapter Outline

Introduction	179
Defining planning for play	180
Reasons for planning play	180
The planning for play continuum	181
Key principles for planning children's learning through play	181
The planning for play process	184
Summary, Jargon Explained, Further Reading, References	196

Introduction

> A key process in teaching is deciding what to do next. This includes responding to children's initiatives, taking the initiative, changing the direction, intervening. In many contexts this is called planning, but *deciding* also includes intuitive and spontaneous responding (Carr 2001: 158).

This chapter will look at what is involved in planning. It will draw on what you have learned about effective play provision, adult intervention and monitoring and assessment and how you can ensure each of these aspects takes place in a coordinated way.

Purpose of this chapter

To help you understand:

- the importance of planning for play
- the role of the practitioner in planning for play
- the process of planning for play

Activity 10.1: Personal learning journal

Purpose: To understand how individual children's concerns and interests can be identified in preparation for planning.

- Make an observation of your target child. Identify a particular concern or interest, which she demonstrates in her play. Note in which provision area(s) this takes place and the actions she performs in each area. Note whether there is a particular aspect of learning or development being addressed as part of her play.
- Think about, and make notes on, the changes to provision you would make to accommodate her interest and enhance her experience. Complete the first section of a personal learning journal record sheet. You will return to this at the end of the chapter.
- Keep your observation and now read the rest of the chapter.

Further activity

Re-read the sections on modes of learning and schema in Chapter 2. Make notes on how your target child represents her learning. Can you identify any schema?

Defining planning for play

Planning is a tool that supports practitioners in deciding what action to take. Planning should be embedded into practice and based on assessment. It is part of the observation, assessment, planning and intervention cycle. There are several elements involved, from planning the basic environment and broad themes, to the spontaneous intervention in a child's play. It can be a complex process but one that should be made manageable through having a clear understanding of when and why we plan and what is involved.

Reasons for planning play

We plan to ensure progression, effective use of materials and practitioner involvement in children's learning. As well as skill development, knowledge and understanding, if play is an 'approach to action' (Bruner, see Chapter 5), then we should be planning with children's dispositions and action behaviours in mind. This requires planning an exciting, stimulating and challenging but supportive environment, which ensures play experiences meet children's needs. Planning also helps practitioners in deciding how they can best support children in their play.

The planning for play continuum

There is a continuum of planning adopted in early years settings, from planning a rich learning environment to planning support to meet children's individual needs, as can be seen in Table 10.1.

Table 10.1 The planning for play continuum

Planning a rich learning environment in which children can be motivated and challenged	Planning a range of themes that will provide the children with interesting things to think about	Planning materials and first-hand experiences for each theme	Planning for adults to observe and interact whilst children are playing	Planning support to meet children's individual needs: changes, enhancement, intervention

General ◄――――――――――――――――――――――――――――► Specific

Planning involves keeping the following three elements in mind:

- *Our knowledge and understanding of children*, their interests, how they think, learn and develop and influences that may impact upon their learning
- *Learning/developmental outcomes*, which involve the skills and knowledge we want children to acquire and develop
- *The play environment* we wish to provide that will enable children to pursue and extend their interests, develop skills and knowledge, challenge their thinking and play in different ways

Key principles for planning children's learning through play

The following is a set of key principles or guidelines, which will help you in developing planning in your setting.

Principle 1

There is a shared agreement and understanding amongst the practitioners of the strategies and systems for planning.

There needs to be a policy that clearly sets out the planning process: who will do what, when and how. It should be an agreed policy for which everyone takes ownership and should include guidelines for implementation. It should reflect the individuality of your setting, your values and your philosophy about play and what you are aiming to achieve through your planning. Your planning should be manageable, realistic and monitored.

Principle 2

Planning is one part of the observation, monitoring, assessment and intervention cycle.

Planning is the decision-making process that gathers information from observations, monitoring and assessment and is used as a vehicle to extend children's interests, develop their skills and knowledge, enrich their learning experiences, challenge their thinking and ensure coverage of developmental and learning outcomes. It should include evaluations of the play environment and how children operate within it and therefore any enhancements or changes.

> Good planning is the key to making children's learning effective, exciting, varied and progressive (DfES 2007: 12).

Principle 3

Planning is about ensuring continuity and progression in children's learning.

The practitioner's aims are for children to be deeply involved for long periods of engagement and to develop knowledge and skills in a range of social and curriculum contexts and for play to become more complex. Planning therefore needs to be flexible in order to respond to new learning possibilities as they emerge, taking account of the individual rates at which children learn and the fluid nature of their play. Planned play experiences should offer challenge, the opportunity to integrate existing learning in order to understand new learning and engage the whole child. The maturity and experience of the child (whether they are likely to play in cooperative groups, solitary or parallel play) should also be considered.

Planning for challenge involves setting up activities that offer an appropriate amount of difficulty and puzzlement, promote problem solving and provide opportunity for children to work collaboratively in order to co-construct their ideas. Practitioners should also plan for complexity of thinking and language by asking the question 'how will this activity challenge children's thinking and what level of language will it promote?'

Providing opportunity to integrate existing learning in order to understand new learning requires planning a range of provision and experiences that allow children to explore their interests in a variety of contexts, develop a range of skills and extend and communicate their knowledge. For example, children are very interested in water flowing through a variety of tubes, containers, funnels and in particular the water wheel. The practitioner plans to move the water wheel to the sand so the children can experience the differences and similarities. Planning should also take account of the fact that children learn concepts by going through the three modes of learning (enactive, iconic, symbolic) and by representing their learning in a variety of ways.

Engaging the whole child requires planning an environment that allows children to become deeply involved, use all their senses and play for sustained periods of time. The environment should include opportunity for children to re-visit and develop aspects of their play (spiral curriculum). Where play allows children to be appropriately challenged, then motivation, concentration and perseverance are encouraged.

Figure 10.1 Planning a rich environment in which children can be motivated and challenged, and play for sustained periods

Principle 4

The planning process should include and value the thoughts and viewpoints of all practitioners, children, parents and carers.

Children should have the opportunity to take control over the pace and focus of their learning and be involved in deciding what happens next. Practitioners therefore need planned opportunity to work with the children, both as individuals and in small groups, to discuss and review learning. This involves becoming part of their play, looking at and talking about their work through photographs, models, drawings and taking notes and keeping records (see Chapter 7).

Sharing observations and the positive aspects of children's learning with parents and carers enables them to be more involved in the children's interests and achievements. Asking them about the children's interests at home and taking account of those interests in weekly planning will be of value to the child.

Principle 5

Practitioners are highly skilled in the observation, monitoring, assessment, intervention and planning process.

Practitioners need to be proficient in the three elements of planning (knowledge and understanding of the children, learning and developmental outcomes and the play environment) in order to fully support children in their learning. They require sound knowledge and understanding of child development and how children think and learn within a social context. Their subject knowledge should be good, in order to make the curriculum meaningful and accessible to young learners, and they need to know how to apply this knowledge and understanding in developing a supportive and enriching play environment (Sylva et al. 2004; Siraj-Blatchford et al. 2002). Their disposition should be such that they are reflective, enquiring and seeking to improve their skills in understanding children, taking responsibility for their own professional development.

Opportunities for systematic meaningful observations and assessments need planning into the daily routine. Regular meetings (weekly and daily) to reflect and share information as well as plan future learning and play provision need to take place. There should also be a planned programme of professional development activities.

The planning for play process

The planning process involves making decisions about when and how we plan at each stage of the continuum. The following outlines what is involved and will help with your decisions.

Yearly planning

This focuses on broad curriculum intentions, the stimuli for creating an initial interest and the physical play environment. Yearly planning may be based on:

- knowledge and understanding of how children learn, think and develop
- broad key themes that can be used as starting points – these themes come from past observations of children and the things in which we know they have always been interested. The themes are a stimulus for learning and thinking and not an imposed curriculum
- practitioner knowledge and understanding of the spiral curriculum and her ability to make the difficult aspects of a concept accessible to the children

Each of the key themes should be broad enough to ensure learning and developmental outcomes can be met. These themes can be allocated periods of time. Yearly planning therefore needs to:

- involve planning the basic play provision, which will remain continuous across the year, for example, water, sand and construction (Chapter 8 also supports you in planning provision areas)
- provide a range of possible stimuli within each theme, for example, visits, key artefacts, visitors, which should be interesting, purposeful and relate to the children

Weekly planning

This is based on:

- one theme from the yearly plan and relevant stimuli – this theme may vary in duration, for example, one to two weeks or four to six weeks
- the children's interests, achievements and developmental needs identified through observations
- the children's response to the weekly stimulus, which will change across the course of the weeks
- new, unexpected interests and opportunities presented by the children
- learning/developmental outcomes outlined in the framework to which you work

Weekly planning needs to:

- be agreed at weekly meetings, where a review of practitioners' assessments of children's learning within the contexts provided for them will inform decisions about how existing plans will change for the following week
- consider how the continuous play provision will be enhanced in line with the stimulus and the children's interests, learning and needs
- provide direct teaching according to the theme or planned curriculum intentions and the children's interests, learning and needs

Case Study 10.1: Changes made to weekly planning

The planned theme was On the Move and during the week a fire engine visited the pre-school (planned stimulus). The children's play as a result of this visit was very absorbed with taking journeys to houses and putting out fires. They were also very enthusiastic about the firemen's bell and sirens as well as exploring tubes and pipes to squirt water. It was decided to allow this play to continue into the following week, instead of the planned new stimulus, by introducing a wider range of pipes and tubing in the outdoor water and a collection of bells, horns and sirens as a table-top exploration activity.

Daily planning

Daily planning is about building on children's achievements from the previous day and meeting individual needs. This planning is based on:

- the practitioners' response to their direct intervention and observations of the children
- children's interests, concerns and developmental needs
- curriculum intentions for the week and the children's response to any stimuli
- practitioner knowledge and understanding of how children learn and develop, together with their own personal knowledge and understanding of the world

Case Study 10.2: Changes made to daily planning

We will return to the example of Beth in Chapter 9: 'When is the best time to intervene in play?' In the water tray children were playing with transparent tubes of various sizes. They were using funnels and pushing the tubes up to the tap and watching them fill. Beth in particular became very interested in the water levels in the tubes. She took various tubes of water outside and was fascinated to watch the water stay level as she tilted the tube until eventually it poured out. The practitioner observed this and decided to add colour to the water the next day. This made it easier to see the water levels in the tubes and the effect of surface tension, which the child called 'the bubble on the top'.

Daily planning therefore needs to:

- be flexible to take account of the spontaneous, evaluative decisions practitioners make according to what the children reveal. It may even be appropriate to abandon the daily plan because the children become totally immersed in something else
- be accessible and in a simple format, in order to be a useful working document
- be within the general planning framework for the week
- incorporate the opportunity for practitioners to work with the children in discussing and reviewing their learning. This may include making assessment notes or records and changing planning documentation
- provide for focused teaching and sustained shared thinking

Figure 10.2 Children continue to explore texture and colour. Daily planning needs to take account of children's interest from the previous session

Spontaneous planning

Spontaneous planning is based on contemporaneous decisions to change something, follow a different course of action or add a resource to that which was already in the daily planning. This planning is based on:

- the ad hoc, spontaneous decisions practitioners make from having directly interacted and observed children at play. It may not be documented until the end of the day when practitioners discuss the changes they made and why

- the practitioner's increasing knowledge and understanding of how individual children learn, think and develop
- the practitioner's ability to observe and interact with children in a way that enables them to identify children's interests, thought processes, skills and knowledge
- the practitioner's ability to reflect and act on this information within a short time frame, in order to enrich the children's play and enhance their learning
- the practitioner becoming directly involved in children's play to offer cognitive challenge

The reflection on a day's planning may reveal something very different from the original intentions, as the direction of the play is in the control of the children.

Case Study 10.3: An example of spontaneous planning

A child is playing in the malleable materials area. She has chosen to work with playdough and selects a range of tools including patty tins. She works carefully and alone for a sustained period of time using a variety of cutters to make shapes and place these into the patty tins. She then proceeds to put the tins into a pretend oven. After a while she takes the patty tin to the practitioner and says, 'Would you like one of my lovely cakes?' The practitioner talks with her about how she has made her 'cakes'. The child is quite explicit about the cake-making process so the practitioner asks, 'Would you like to make some real cakes?' This prompts immediate enthusiasm; the child takes control in that she explains to the practitioner what she will need and together they start to make some basic sponge cakes (basic baking materials are always to hand as it is recognized that cooking is an essential part of provision) with the child directing the adult. The practitioner could have chosen to pursue malleable materials or the role play with the child but she tuned in to the enthusiasm and the detail with which the child discussed her pretend cakes. By asking the question, 'Would you like to make some real cakes?' she gave the child choice.

It is important that the team engage in dialogue about all aspects of the planning process and devise systems and pro forma that meet the needs of their individual context.

The daily planning pro forma should be completed at the end of the day for the following day and changes to be made noted. The following are guidelines for devising a daily planning pro forma relevant to your context. It should provide information on:

- changes to the physical layout of the setting
- key events or aspects of routine relevant to the day/session
- enhanced learning opportunities based on new knowledge of the children's interests and needs

(remember this is about changes or additions you might make to the experience or provision but is not about telling the children what to do)

- what each practitioner will be doing to support the children, where and with whom, for example, who will be making observations, who will be outdoors, who will meet and greet, who will be involved in focused activities

In preparation for the next activity, return to your notes from Activity 10.1 in which you thought about what changes to provision you would make to accommodate your target child's interest and enhance their experience.

The following activities will take you through the planning process. This will require discussion, reflection and refining and take a period of time. This is because you are developing a high quality learning context in which children can operate at their highest level.

Activity 10.2: Yearly planning: planning provision as part of the learning environment

In Chapter 8 you carried out Activity 8.1, which enhanced an area of provision. Remind yourself of this activity in preparation for the team meeting.

This activity will enable you to decide as a team which areas of provision you will make continuous. You will need to refer to Chapter 8: 'What makes a quality play environment: key principles', and the example of a provision area plan, referred to in Chapter 8 and Table 8.1. In particular you will need to consider the following for each provision area:

- where you will site the area
- space allocation you will give to the area
- boundary demarcation for the area
- structural or large equipment (such as a water tray) that is a permanent feature of the area

Activity 10.3: Yearly planning: themes

As a team decide upon the broad themes you will use as starting points for thinking and learning across the year. You will need a minimum of six themes. Remember they need to be about what the children find interesting, for example, On the Move.

For each area, plan some appropriate stimuli, for example, a visit to a railway museum, a day where the children bring in bicycles from home or arrange a fire-engine to visit your setting and some key additional resources.

Activity 10.4: Yearly planning: children's learning and development in the theme

As a team take one theme and think about the learning opportunities you might provide for each of the areas of learning and development: mathematical, linguistic, physical, creative, knowledge and understanding and social. Refer to Table 8.1 in Chapter 8. Consider how you will record this aspect of planning. You may present your planning in the following format or decide upon an alternative.

Figure 10.3 is an example of a pro forma you might use for planning for children's learning and development as part of a theme.

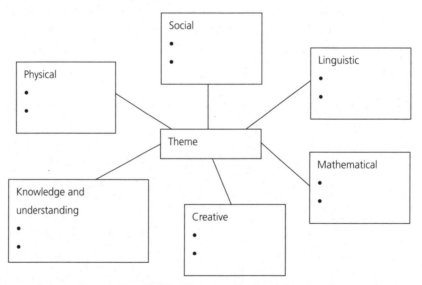

Figure 10.3 Planning for children's learning and development as part of a theme

Activity 10.4 (continued)

As you do this, check against the Early Years Framework to which you work. Make adjustment if you find there are some areas of learning and development you have not addressed or there is an unequal balance.

Activity 10.5: Yearly planning: planning provision as part of the theme and stimuli

As a team take one theme and consider how you might change and enhance each provision area to support learning across the theme. You will need to think about stimulus, resources, language and the role of the adult as well as indoor and outdoor provision areas.

Figure 10.4 is an example of a pro forma you might use for planning for provision as part of a theme and stimuli.

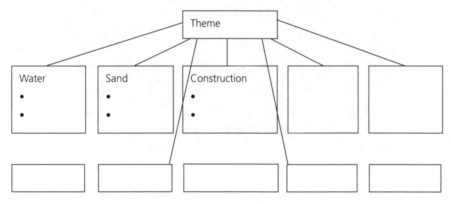

Figure 10.4

Further activity

As a team decide for how long you will trial your planning methods and recording pro forma and how and when you will evaluate them. Consider together how you will record your decisions. Design pro forma that are simple, clear and yet contain the required information that will suit your way of working. Figure 10.4 is an example.

Activity 10.5 (continued)

Evaluate your planning by considering:

- the extent to which you took into account the influences upon children's development and learning as described in Chapter 3 (re-visit your ideas map that you made in Activity 3.2)
- the key ideas, which inform us about learning through play, as discussed in Chapter 4
- the usefulness and practicalities of the planning pro forma you devised

Figure 10.5 Enhancing a provision area to support children's learning and development

Activity 10.6: Weekly planning

Purpose: To understand the process of planning for children's concerns and interests.

Take a theme from the yearly planning and consider its intended duration (one or two weeks, four or five weeks etc.). Think about what interest and stimulus you will have for each week (this may be the same theme as Activity 10.5).

Start to implement your theme by deciding how you will enhance each provision area and your learning intentions for each week. Refer to Table 8.1 in Chapter 8, 'Provision area enhancement', to help you.

Activity 10.7: Weekly planning

Your team meeting needs to take place towards the end of the week and you need to use the 'Framework for discussion in weekly planning meetings' (see below) as a guide.

Each practitioner needs to come prepared with records of observation(s) of their key children from the current week.

You are now going to plan for next week. You will already have in place your intended focus and learning intentions for the week (see Activity 10.6 above). You are now going to incorporate your information about children's specific interests.

First, consider each practitioner's observation(s). From what has been presented about the children, identify any common interests, achievements and developmental needs. Consider children's response to the planned theme and stimuli so far. Identify any new, unexpected opportunities presented by the children. Identify any opportunities for group work whether child- or practitioner-led.

Now reflect on your original intentions and stimulus for next week and in light of your discussion decide how you will enhance the provision areas in order to enrich, extend and support the children's particular interests. This may mean making considerable changes to your original plans. Think about the resources, language, whether you will change or add to the specific intended stimuli and the role of the practitioners.

At the end of next week reflect on the changes and your attempts to enhance the provision according to the children's interests and needs.

Activity 10.8: Daily planning: Planning in response to children's interests, concerns and achievements

As an individual, reflect on some aspect of an individual child's play where you made a decision to intervene based upon an observation or as a result of your interaction with the child. Note down the following:

- the action you took, modelling, drawing attention, asking a question, adding or changing a resource, making a suggestion, shared sustained thinking
- how your action extended and enriched the child's learning
- the social context in which the play was taking place
- the response of the child to your intervention

Activity 10.8 (continued)

Reflect on the effect of your intervention, in other words, did your intervention support, enrich or extend the child's learning, and consider the best course of action for continuing to support the child? Decide what you think needs to change in the planning for the following day based on your reflection and considerations. Use Chapter 9 to help you.

Team meeting

- Each person feeds back to the team
- Use the 'Framework for discussion in daily planning meetings' (see below) for your discussion
- The team now decides how they will develop planning for the following day based on the new knowledge of the children

Further activity

Each member of the group evaluates other recording methods, from different sources, in light of the information you have gathered in this chapter. Using this information decide, 'What does the team need to do next in order to improve planning for play?'

Activity 10.9: Personal learning journal

This activity involves the completing of a personal learning journal record sheet.

Return to Activity 10.1, in which you observed and made notes on the changes to provision you would make for your target child to accommodate her interests and enhance her experience. You completed the first section of a personal learning journal record sheet. Now continue to complete the sheet. In the second section reflect on your learning about planning from this chapter. Review and analyse your notes, in the light of your new learning and refine your thinking. How well did you consider her needs? How would you make use of this information for planning purposes? At what point in the planning process would you use this information? Is there any other information you need to gather to help you in your understanding about planning for individual concerns and needs? As a key worker with responsibility for a group of children consider what action you will take in the future to improve one aspect of planning in order to meet all their needs, and complete the third section. Implement your action and in the fourth section evaluate its impact by looking at how well the children engaged in their play and how well they progressed in their learning.

The following frameworks support you by providing a focus for discussion in the weekly and daily planning meetings.

Framework for discussion in weekly planning meetings

All practitioners should make sure their views and thoughts are shared at the meeting, whether in person or not.

There should be a review and evaluation of:

- the original intentions and stimulus for the week in terms of curriculum content and children's interests
- the original intentions for the week in terms of the enhanced provision
- additions and changes made to the provision in response to children's ideas/interests/learning
- outcomes from assessments of groups and individuals
- the role and use of adults in supporting/assessing the children's play
- decisions for the following week
- which aspects of the original weekly planning are to remain the same or change based on the children's interests, concerns and needs observed
- what the social contexts and opportunities for peer interaction and collaboration are
- what other information needs to be gathered, e.g. from parents/carers, from the children, from children's previous learning and achievements
- what observations and assessments are to be made across the week
- what direct teaching will take place and what the role of other adults is
- completion of relevant planning pro forma

Framework for discussion in daily planning meetings

Review the Post-its or other notes/records from the day's observations (these may be attached to the daily planning pro forma) for any surprises and significant achievements in the children's learning or development, for example, use of resources, skills, knowledge, thought process, interests, social interactions, attitudes to learning.

There should be a discussion about:

- any overlaps, similarities or conflicts in the children's interests
- the social contexts in which play/learning is taking place and the opportunities for peer interaction and collaboration
- the particular provision areas in which children's interests are developing
- individual children's learning needs

Decisions should be made about:

- what should remain the same for the following day
- how you will meet individual children's learning needs
- what should change for the following day, e.g. resources, language, stimulus
- the practitioners' direct teaching, observations, involvement with the children

Changes should be made to relevant planning pro forma, assessments completed and Post-its or other notes/records filed in children's profiles.

Summary

This chapter has supported you in answering the questions:

- What is planning?
- When do we plan and from where does the planning come?
- Why do we plan and how do we go about it?

You have drawn together your knowledge of the key ideas about children's development and learning, the importance of a rich, stimulating and challenging environment and how adults can best support children's learning.

You should now be ready to develop your planning in a way that you consider meets the needs of your children and provides progression in their learning.

Jargon explained

Cognitive challenge: This is where an activity makes children think but is still achievable.

Further reading

Carr, M. (2001), *Assessment in Early Childhood Settings: Learning Stories.* London: Paul Chapman.
 In this book planning is seen as the fourth element in the Assessment process and asks the question 'what next?' in the child's learning story. The focus is on tracking levels of participation and making decisions about children's 'learning dispositions' or attitudes to learning.

DfES (2007), *The Early Years Foundation Stage: Setting the Standards for Learning, Development and Care for Children from Birth to Five*. DfES.
 These documents set out the statutory framework and the practice guidance for the foundation stage, which ensures children of 0–5 achieve the five Every Child Matters outcomes of staying safe, being

healthy, enjoying and achieving, making a positive contribution, and achieving economic well-being. They set out the requirements for Learning and Development and welfare for children in maintained and non-maintained schools, independent schools and with registered childcare providers. Each of the areas of Learning and Development in appendix 2 of the guidance contains a section on planning and resources. The CD-Rom contains examples of planning pro forma.

Rodger, R. (2003), *Planning an Appropriate Curriculum for the Under Fives: A Guide for Students, Teachers and Assistants.* London: David Fulton.

This book takes each area of learning and provides examples of effective planning supported by case study material. It also looks at the role that monitoring and assessment has in the planning process and considers the writing of an early years policy and curriculum together with aspects of leadership and management.

References

Carr, M. (2001), *Assessment in Early Childhood Settings: Learning Stories.* London: Paul Chapman.

DfES (2007), *Practice Guidance for the Early Years Foundation Stage*, in *The Early Years Foundation Stage: Setting the Standards for Learning, Development and Care for Children from Birth to Five.* DfES.

Siraj-Blatchford, I., Sylva, K., Muttock, S., Gilden, R. and Bell, D. (2002), *Researching Effective Pedagogy in the Early Years* (REPEY). DfES.

Sylva, K., Melhuish, E., Sammons, P., Siraj-Blatchford, I. and Taggart, B. (2004), *The Effective Provision of Pre-School Education Project* (EPPE). DfES.

Part Four

MANAGEMENT, EVALUATION AND DEVELOPMENT OF QUALITY PRE-SCHOOL PROVISION

The Role of the Adult: Leadership and Management

11

Chapter Outline

Introduction   201
The role of the practitioner in leading and managing learning through
    play   202
Key principles and frameworks for the effective management and
    leadership of learning through play   204
Summary, Jargon explained, Further reading, References   218

Introduction

Although this chapter is aimed at practitioners who have, or anticipate they will have, management responsibilities in a pre-school, it will also explore the development of adult relationships, team working and management of the observation, assessment, planning and intervention cycle. Some consideration will be given to working with parents.

We know from research that children make better progress in all aspects of development and learning in settings where there is strong leadership (Sylva et al. 2004; Siraj-Blatchford et al. 2002). This strong leadership is more than the implementation of systems or the organization and monitoring of staff and play activities associated with management. It relates to building and maintaining the setting's ethos, its social, cultural and learning climate, the communication of shared values regarding play and children's learning and the effectiveness of the adults in their engagement with the children.

The leaders involved in the research of Aubrey et al. (2006) considered the delivery of a quality service the most important aspect of their role. We know that where there is a balance between self-initiated and self-managed activities, and playful teaching, then children are more likely to achieve their best. Such contexts are created by a consistent and strong team of knowledgeable, well-trained practitioners who form genuine interactive relationships with children based upon an informed understanding of their social and cognitive development (Sylva et al. 2004; Siraj-Blatchford et al. 2002; Siraj-Blatchford and Manni 2006).

Day et al. (2000) in their research into head teacher effectiveness concluded that the effectiveness with which people are managed, motivated and developed is fundamental to improving performance. Both Aubrey et al. (2006) and Rodd (1998) talk of the strong teams that exist in early childhood settings, teams that work collaboratively and inspire and motivate each other to achieve their goals.

Purpose of this chapter

To help you understand:

- what is involved in leading and managing learning through play
- what is involved in providing a quality service
- what is involved in leading and managing effective teams

The role of the practitioner in leading and managing learning through play

The assumption that managers will work as part of the early years team, in carrying out activities and reflecting on their own practice, has underpinned this book. The continuum of play leadership starts with a strong vision, which is shared by a team of skilled practitioners and effectively communicated to parents, carers and the children. This is translated into a set of achievable goals with systems and procedures that support the team in achieving the shared vision. A team that engages in collective reflection, reciprocal learning and is supported in taking a lead role in the management of play at some point of the process, is at the other end of the continuum. The leader therefore requires a sound understanding of how children learn through their play experiences to facilitate this and how the practitioners should operate within the environment. They should also understand the principles of effective leadership and possess particular characteristics, which will enable the team to give of their best for the children's benefit.

Activity 11.1: Personal learning journal

Purpose: To reflect upon your characteristics as a leader and manager of your setting by considering how you deal with key issues.

You will return to this activity at the end of the chapter to reconsider your answers and further action, so you need to decide in what format you might record your reflections. In this activity you are asked to spend time answering the following questions, which encourage you to think about your current practice in terms of key issues, such as standards for play, relationships, teamwork, communication, monitoring and evaluation:

- How do you go about defining and setting standards for high quality play?
- How do you build and strengthen relationships and the professional team, in order to develop the play environment and children's learning?
- How often do you become involved in the work of the team and what role do you take?
- What are the roles and responsibilities of practitioners for developing play? How is this shared with everyone?
- Do you have a policy and action plan for the development of play? If so, then you may like to re-read it at this point and consider any changes you would make in light of the work you have done in this book
- What systems do you have for communication in your setting and how effective are they?
- To what extent do you and your staff engage in the process of self-evaluation, as individuals and as a team, through observation, reflection, action and evaluation?
- In what ways do you spend time in developing your expertise in understanding children's play and learning and the expertise of the practitioners? This might include looking beyond your setting at others' practice and at relevant research
- What strategies do you currently use for monitoring and evaluating the quality of the play environment, quality of children's learning and the role of the practitioner?
- How do you recognize and acknowledge the achievement of individual practitioners and the team in developing the play environment and enhancing children's learning and give credit where credit is due?
- How do you celebrate success together and share that success with children, parents/carers and the wider community?

The purpose of this book is to improve the quality of play in your setting, in other words, the play environment, play experiences, children's learning and the role of the practitioner in supporting children's play. In order to do this a strategy or 'plan of action' needs to be in place. Improving play in your context, however, will be considered more closely in Chapter 12; first you need to consider some key principles and look more closely at developing strong teamwork.

Key principles and frameworks for the effective management and leadership of learning through play

The following is a set of key principles that should underpin play practice in your setting and help you later in forming your strategy. The associated frameworks provide guidance in developing that aspect of your practice which is your leadership and management role, in other words, 'What do I need to put in place and how do I go about it?'

Principle 1: There is a shared vision and values for play

> Leaders who delivered and encouraged effective communication amongst and between staff were found capable of ensuring that the vision of the setting, in regards to practice, policy and processes, infiltrated the whole ethos of a centre; promoting consistency amongst staff working with children and families (Siraj-Blatchford and Manni 2006: 17).

Where there is a shared vision and ownership of the goals then staff feel empowered, motivated and energized to work together to achieve those goals (Day et al. 2000; Rodd 1998).

Developing and providing high quality play is the core work of any early years setting. Quality cannot be achieved on an ad hoc, inconsistent basis; there needs to be a common approach based upon a set of shared principles. It is about deciding what you consider to be important in terms of the play environment and experiences and children's learning and development and continually reminding yourself of this.

A set of clearly defined, co-constructed goals for developing all aspects of play ensures common understanding, direction and purpose for the team. Co-constructed means all practitioners have explored their own values and then constructed a set of values together, which support them in articulating and justifying their practice and providing a consistent message about the importance of learning through play with parents and carers.

A manager who consistently sets standards for high quality play and engages in dialogue with the team provides a good role model.

A strong vision for learning through play forms a basis on which the setting can accept new ideas and externally imposed initiatives. It enables the setting to manage change.

Principle 2: Practitioners know and understand how children learn and develop through play

> Effective practitioners use their own learning to improve their work with young children and their families in ways which are sensitive, positive and non-judgemental (DfES 2005: 3).

A strong commitment to Continuing Professional Development is recognized as a means of achieving the goals of the setting. In promoting professional growth a culture of reflective practice is established, where practitioners are constantly required to review and analyse their own experiences, interactions and understanding of children's learning and the play environment. Deeper insight into their practice gives practitioners the confidence to talk in an informed manner, carry out action research into some aspect of children's play that interests them, observe their peers interacting with children and implement and evaluate new ideas.

In Reggio Emilia, professional development is:

> ...considered to be a continuing evolutionary process that is an intrinsic part of the teacher's day. At its heart is the belief in staff development as *change*; staff development as promoting *participation and interaction* (Early Education Support 2006: 20).

The role of the manager is to ensure that embedded into the daily/weekly practice is the opportunity for all practitioners, including themselves, to meet with colleagues for meaningful discussion, carry out systematic observations and assessments and take part in practitioner enquiry.

Framework for facilitating practitioner learning

This framework is a set of ideas to support you in your role as facilitator of practitioner learning and in creating a climate of review and evaluation.

- Be a role model in the process of observation, reflection, analysis, action and evaluation, for example, by setting up and taking part in a system of peer observation, review and evaluation, where the practitioners observe each other when interacting in some aspect of the children's play. This informs individual personal learning but also the work of the team
- Ask questions of others such as how do you think you could have done that better? Why did you do it in that way? How would you do things differently? What would happen if...? Have you thought about...? This can be done formally and informally and encourage practitioners to articulate their thinking and justify their actions, using appropriate language
- Remind practitioners of what they already know, understand, value and do well in terms of developing play experiences, supporting children's learning and working with parents and carers.

This means keeping the elements of your vision in mind and monitoring practitioners' work

- Provide opportunities to talk, share ideas, solve problems but with an agreed focus. This is where your development plan for play provides you with a range of aspects on which to focus (see Chapter 12)

- Monitor the practice of individuals and the team, through observing, questioning and discussing their work. This will enable you to support them in exploring and identifying key issues for development and breaking those issues down into manageable parts to solve in stages. Referring to the vision helps in identifying issues. Implementing action plans provides momentum. This is very similar to 'scaffolding' children's learning

- Spend time in coaching, encouraging, inviting and giving feedback, in order for practitioners to succeed and do a good job. Practitioners who are given responsibilities and encouraged to take a lead should be provided with the necessary support in order to meet their new demands. For example, in supporting an individual in taking responsibility for the evaluation and development of a particular aspect of the play provision you would need to provide training but, in return, expect regular feedback on progress and impact on children's learning. Making use of staff expertise to take a lead in some aspect of play not only empowers that person, but can also lead to improvement in the quality of her learning.

Case Study 11.1

The following is an example of how one manager influenced the practice of others through direct involvement and role modelling.

The manager of a setting valued role play as a means of developing children's language and communication skills through shared dialogue based upon children's own ideas and experiences. Role play, however, was usually set up around a particular inflexible theme, for example, a fairy tale, and allowed little opportunity for the children to 'act out' their own ideas and personal experiences. During her time away from management tasks the manager made a point of working in the role-play area with the children. She developed her own skills of interacting with children, including shared sustained thinking. She was able to monitor the opportunities for skill and cognitive and affective development the role play provided. She was able to consider the breadth and depth of the children's play. This took place over a period of four weeks and enabled the manager to have in-depth discussion with the team. By engaging in this way a range of things could be achieved with the team:

- Raising the status of this provision area in the eyes of the other practitioners and the children. More boys became involved in the role play and practitioners developed a rota/timetable so they could all have the opportunity, during the course of a week, to play alongside the children in this area

Case Study 11.1 (continued)

- Influencing practice by role-modelling how the practitioners might engage with children in role play and shared sustained thinking but also modelling the role of the adult as a learner. This resulted in a discussion about the benefits but also the difficulties and skills required in shared sustained thinking
- It enabled her to ask in-depth questions of the team in order to encourage reflection on what they might develop and how. In this case they discussed how all the areas of learning were met through the opportunities offered, how they could ensure children sustained their play and how as adults they would intervene
- She was able to offer feedback to the team on how play was developing and how children's language and communication were improving. It also enabled her to involve the staff in an informed dialogue, in which everyone, through their experience, was able to contribute

As a result one of the practitioners decided to use the role-play area for her own piece of action research, with a view to improving her own skills and understanding in shared sustained thinking and the quality of the children's imaginative language.

Principle 3: There is a strong sense of collegiality where practitioners work as a team to develop the play environment and experiences

> …the essence of a team is that all participants work together effectively to achieve a common goal (Rodd 1998: 99).

Research shows that in early childhood settings, with high quality leadership, there is a strong sense of collegiality and collaborative working. In addition, where there is recognition by the leader that the team collectively has a wealth of specialist knowledge and expertise and that a range of individuals may take part in and contribute to leadership activity this can lead to 'concertive action' by the setting (Bennett et al. 2003; Aubrey et al. 2006).

Framework for developing team work

In order for teams to function they need to be aware of the skills and actions that they need to develop. This framework is a set of ideas to support you in facilitating effective teamwork.

- Defining, understanding and sharing roles and responsibilities, for example, for planning, setting up and monitoring aspects of the play environment and the roles of key practitioners
- Ensuring open communication, where everyone feels they can contribute without judgement or 'put down'. This involves mutual respect and a valuing of each other's contributions and a leader who promotes effective communication amongst practitioners. It also requires individuals to understand their actions may have consequences for others
- Encouraging and enabling the team to take a lead in exploring issues, making decisions and taking action, whether in small groups or the whole team. This will emerge from shared activity and dialogue within a context of openness, mutual trust and support and from shared goals and values. It requires a recognition on your part that individuals in the team have a range of knowledge, expertise and perspectives that when put together means action can have a greater impact (Bennett et al. 2003)
- Creating opportunities for practitioners to work together in new ways. Where a manager is creative and makes use of the collective knowledge base and challenges the status quo, this empowers practitioners to be creative in their thinking and practice. They are able to do things differently to meet the specific needs of the children and families within the setting more effectively (Siraj-Blatchford and Manni 2006)
- Collaborating and agreeing outcomes. This involves finding ways of setting time aside for the team to work together. Collaboration can reduce workload, make use of the wealth of shared expertise, give confidence to individuals and provide the basis for a learning community

Figure 11.1 The work of the team is to consider resources and materials that meet their children's interests and needs. What decisions might your team make in regard to this provision area?

Activity 11.2: Personal learning journal

Purpose: To reflect on your role as facilitator during a team meeting.

This activity will begin to help you in understanding the characteristics of leadership and management involved in facilitating effective teamwork.

Choose a team meeting, from one of the professional development activities you have recently led, that you feel it would be useful to analyse. Analyse the meeting, using a personal learning journal record sheet, from two points of view: the quality of participation and interaction of the practitioners and how well you supported the discussion.

Description of the meeting

Write a brief description of the meeting. Describe the focus for discussion and any agreed outcomes.

Reflection on the meeting

Analyse the meeting under the following headings:

Quality of participation and interaction of the practitioners

Consider the following:

- the extent to which each member of the team participated; the type of contribution made to the discussion; who took the lead in discussion; who took a supporting role; who provided alternative viewpoints; the level of respect, active listening, knowledge and expertise demonstrated
- the level of reflection and analysis that took place; level of description and anecdote; scrutiny of 'how' and 'why'; the extent to which previous experience and other evidence was used; identification of strengths and areas for development

How well you supported the team

Consider the following:

- To what extent did you enable and encourage the team to take the lead and discuss freely amongst themselves or were most of their comments directed through yourself?
- To what extent did your comments or questions promote reflection and criticality amongst the team?
- How did you ensure the team stayed focused on the task in hand and the outcomes?
- What conclusions did they arrive at for themselves?
- How well did you listen?

Activity 11.2 (continued)

- In what ways did you remind the team of their strengths, achievements, knowledge, skills and understanding?

Is there other information you need to help you with your reflection, for example, information regarding children, minutes of previous meetings, further reading on play to be sure of your knowledge and understanding? The role of manager can feel very isolated; it is therefore useful to cultivate a working relationship with a manager of another setting who will act as 'buddy' or coaching partner. Are there any questions you would like to ask a critical friend? Use this information to help you refine your thinking.

Information from other sources helps you in clarifying your thoughts and defining issues. The perspective of other colleagues also helps you to consider a different viewpoint.

Consider the following:

- Has your thinking changed from your original analysis, and in what way?
- Did you have an emotional response to the meeting, and if so in what way has that changed?
- What have you learned so far about the team and yourself?

Action

Consider the question 'What will I do differently?' in terms of the quality of participation and interaction of the practitioners and how well you supported the discussion. Remember that your long-term aim is to create a strong sense of collegiality, where practitioners collaborate and work effectively together to develop the play environment and play experiences. In addition, can you identify ways in which the team could work together differently in order to be more creative in their thinking and practice?

Decide upon your action in terms of what changes you will make to your performance in order to improve the participation and interaction of the practitioners. You will need to consider what preparations to make for the next team meeting.

Evaluation

There are three things that need monitoring and evaluating: your action in terms of supporting the team, the performance of the team and the impact on the children's play experiences and learning.

Continue to keep notes in your personal learning journal of future team meetings.

Principle 4: Parents/carers and the wider community are seen as offering a valid contribution to enhancing play

Finding ways in which children's learning can be enhanced and supported is paramount. Parents have a wealth of knowledge about their children's development and learning, which practitioners need to draw upon. Parents are more likely to become involved with and have a positive attitude towards the work of the setting if they understand the importance of play in children's learning and development. Practitioners can only be proactive in supporting parents in understanding what and how their children are learning if they have a clear understanding of the process themselves. It is important that parents hear the same message and it is consistently spoken. Where practitioners are competent and confident they are more likely to welcome and involve parents in the day-to-day work of the setting.

Principle 5: Systems and procedures support the work of the team in developing play

We have established that a strong vision for play together with confident and competent practitioners supports the identification of goals to be achieved. Systems and procedures should be enabling in that they support the practitioners in achieving those goals. Below is an overview of leadership and management activity during the course of a year, for planning, intervention, monitoring and assessment of play. You will, however, develop your own time line based upon your context. The team will carry out most of the work but there will be some key activities for which only the manager of the setting can be responsible.

Table 11.1 An overview of leadership and management activity in developing play

Leadership and management activity	What to do	How to do it	When to do it
In addition to the following there should be a policy in place for each leadership and management activity. These policies will include what you will be doing and why but should also contain guidelines against which you can monitor progress and impact. Refer to the Activity 7.1 in Chapter 7 and the Policy for Play in Appendix 1.			
Planning play	Plan the play environment. Plan themes of interest and ensure areas of learning/development are covered.	Whole team planning meeting where the year is reviewed and the following year planned. Prior to the meeting the staff should review children's portfolios and evaluate themes and provision. Planning pro forma completed and displayed for reference.	Yearly meeting, either at end or beginning of year. You will need to decide when your year ends and begins. In school this is obvious.
	Plan stimulus for themes, visits and additional resources and materials.	Team meetings, which are informed by observations and assessments. Timed agenda worked out in advance to ensure focus. These could be 'stand up' meetings. May need a rota of attendance depending on constraints. Pro forma completed and displayed for reference.	Meeting prior to implementation of new theme. Daily meetings of 15 minutes and weekly meetings of 30 minutes at end of week.
Observation, monitoring and assessment of play	Observation and assessment of children.	Rota for staff observation and assessment of key children.	Weekly team meeting.
	Tracking children's progress.	Key practitioners given time to select and review portfolios/ learning journeys of their children for tracking progress against learning/developmental outcomes. Manager works in setting to allow key practitioners opportunity to monitor children's progress.	Rota so each week a key practitioner is given time to track progress.

Table 11.1 (continued)

Leadership and management activity	What to do	How to do it	When to do it
The play environment	Plan the play environment indoors and outdoors.	Whole team planning meeting (see above – Planning play).	Yearly meeting (see above – Planning play).
	Plan additional resources and materials to provide stimulus and meet interests, needs.	Whole team planning meeting.	Weekly and daily meetings (see above – Planning play).
		Review use of resources, children's needs and interests. Prioritize purchase of new resources.	Yearly, weekly and daily in preparation for setting up ongoing and enhanced provision. Prior to budget being set.
		Agree other resources to be gathered and by whom.	Yearly, weekly and daily.
		Staff to agree storage and maintenance responsibilities.	Yearly meeting but the responsibility for monitoring the use and quality may be rotated and discussed at weekly meeting.
	Supervision of children indoors and outdoors.	Agree rota for general supervision of children outdoors and at what point rotation changes according to where the children are choosing to play (predominantly outdoors or indoors).	Weekly meeting but reviewed daily according to weather and children's interests.

Table 11.1 (continued)

Leadership and management activity	What to do	How to do it	When to do it
The work of the team	Define roles and responsibilities including key practitioners.	Roles and responsibilities outlined and agreed on appointment to position.	Induction.
		Sharing and reviewing with the team (some roles and responsibilities may be rotated to ensure equality of opportunity and expertise).	Half-term staff meeting when roles, systems and procedures are discussed.
	Draw up rotas to ensure children are supervised, environment is safe, staff can observe and interact with children, e.g. setting up, clearing away, designated working areas, resources, observations, interaction, direct teaching.	Allocating children to key practitioners. During team meetings draw up lists of activities and create timetables and rota lists for which the team has shared responsibility.	Weekly and daily meetings.
	Professional development takes place to ensure adults know and understand how children learn and develop through play.	Provide opportunities for practising and making observations and assessments, e.g. choosing five children for the week and providing cover for key practitioner to make observations.	Across the week, decided at weekly and daily meetings.
		Regular discussions to define individual needs, skills and interests for staff development.	Allocate your time across the year to observe all staff and hold a meeting to provide feedback and discuss training needs.
		Draw up a policy and system for staff training. Implement and monitor progress against objectives.	Training plan needs to be decided with costs identified prior to budget being set.

Table 11.1 (continued)

Leadership and management activity	What to do	How to do it	When to do it
Working with parents	Gathering information from parents regarding children's play interests and skills.	Key workers of those children chosen for assessment, to discuss play interests with parents, either face to face or through communication books.	Daily, during beginning or end of session. Key practitioners given time to write up communication books and file information into profiles or learning journeys.
	Providing feedback to parents regarding children's learning through play.	Key practitioners give formal feedback to parents/carers at regular update meetings.	Regular meetings planned across the year for parent interviews.
	Providing information about the play environment and experiences.	Your prospectus will contain your policies. Newsletters, parent display and information boards can be a shared responsibility of the team and focus on informing parents why you do things and what and how their children learn as well as information regarding projects and resources to collect.	Newsletters and posters for display board should be changed or sent out on a regular basis, e.g. every half term or start of every theme. You may also, as manager, have a time each week for parents to meet with you.
		Open Days.	One or two open days organized across the year as a sharing and information giving/ promotional event.
	Involvement of parents in children's play and learning.	Inviting parents into setting at beginning and end of the session. Encouraging parents/ carers to stay for part or all of the session and play with the children.	Daily.

Table 11.1 (continued)

Leadership and management activity	What to do	How to do it	When to do it
Action plan for the development of play and re-visiting your vision (see Chapter 12)	Ensure action plans are implemented, monitored and evaluated.	Identify those aspects of the action plan that need to be incorporated into this overview. Monitor progress of action as outlined in action plans and evaluation.	See time frames on action plan. See monitoring and evaluation activity on action plans for dates.
	Review your vision statement.	Your vision for play should be embedded in all the above activity. It is why you are doing things. You should, perhaps at the start of each year, remind yourselves of the key question, 'What do we want for our children?'	When planning, reviewing policies, discussing children's progress, working with parents, team meetings. Yearly review meeting.

Activity 11.3: Team meeting

Purpose: To identify and plan leadership and management activity for you and the team.

This professional development activity will help you in identifying and prioritizing the leadership and management activity that takes place daily/weekly and across the year in order to ensure the development of play.

Preparation:

- Use Table 11.1 and add any additional leadership and management activity that is relevant to your setting
- Take a yearly calendar, divided into months, such as a wall-planner
- Use the overview and map onto your calendar all the activities across the year

Meeting:

- Share and discuss the calendar with the team, especially open days, parent interviews, staff training and so on. Add in any additional activity
- Identify those activities that only you can do, and those activities that can and should be carried out by the team. There will be some overlaps and some things that you need to do in preparation for a team meeting

Activity 11.3 (continued)

- As each month comes along map out your activity, and that of the team, for each week. A designated person may be responsible for drawing up the team's monthly overview
- Work two to three weeks in advance so you are planning ahead as some juggling may be necessary to even out the workload. The aim is to ensure a timetable of activity related to the play environment, play experiences, the children's learning and practitioner activity

This plan of activity will need to be flexible but it should support you in making play your focus for development.

Activity 11.4: Personal learning journal

Purpose: To reflect on your characteristics as a leader and manager by considering how you deal with key issues.

This activity involves completing a personal learning journal record sheet.

- Return to Activity 11.1 in which you were asked to spend time evaluating your current practice in terms of key issues. In the first section of the record sheet, briefly describe the activity. In the second section reflect on your answers and identify any patterns. Decide which aspects of leading and managing the play provision you do well and how do you know?
- Using the information you have gathered from reading and completing the activities in this chapter, reflect upon your answers to the questions and decide which aspects you would change or improve, why and how
- In which aspects do you need to develop your skills, knowledge and expertise and how will you go about this? Complete the 'Action' section of the sheet, outlining what you will do differently
- Under 'Evaluation' develop your personal action plan. You might like to use the headings/pro forma set out in Table 11.2

Table 11.2 An example of a pro forma for a personal development action plan

Personal Development Action Plan				
Name:		Time frame:		
Aspect for improvement	Action	Support	When	Evaluation and evidence
I want to be able to……..	I will achieve it by doing……..	I will need support from…….. (person or other)	I will achieve it by……..	I am doing well at…….. My evidence is……..
Review date:		Next steps:		

Summary

In this chapter we have demonstrated the importance of forming positive, working relationships and developing a strong team who are committed to personal professional growth. Ensuring shared values and communicating a strong vision for play is the key to improving the quality of play in your setting. Involving parents is an important factor in enhancing the play experiences of children.

You should now be able to:

- understand your role within the practitioner team and the personal characteristics you need to continue to develop, in order to facilitate collegiality and practitioner learning
- plan your leadership and management activity to ensure the development of play in your setting

You should now be ready to move on to the final chapter, which supports you in developing and communicating a vision, action planning, evaluating practice and personal development planning.

Jargon explained

Concertive action: This is where a group of people bring together their expertise and initiative to work in such a way that their combined energy is 'greater than the sum of their individual actions' (Bennett et al. 2003).

Further reading

DfES (2005), *Key Elements of Effective Practice* (KEEP). DfES.

  KEEP is a framework for effective practice, taken from the Principles for Early Education and based upon the REPEY (2002), EPPE (2004) and SPEEL (2002) research. It recognizes that effective learning is based upon practitioners forming 'secure relationships, an appropriate learning environment and high quality teaching'. It states that in order to do these, practitioners must: understand how children develop and learn, have good subject knowledge and develop the curriculum, be able to use a range of teaching and intervention strategies, and support child-initiated learning. Ongoing training and development is therefore important if practitioners are to continue to improve.

DfES (2007), *Statutory Framework and Practice Guidance for the Foundation Stage: Setting the Standards for Learning, Development and Care for Children from Birth to Five*. DfES.

  This document sets out the statutory framework and the practice guidance for the foundation stage, which ensures children of 0–5 achieve the five Every Child Matters outcomes of staying safe, being healthy, enjoying and achieving, making a positive contribution, and achieving economic well-being. It sets out the requirements for learning and development and welfare for children in maintained and non-maintained schools, independent schools and with registered childcare providers.

Moyles, J., Adams, S. and Musgrove, A. (2002), *SPEEL: A Study of Pedagogical Effectiveness in Early Learning*. DfES.

  The Framework for Effective Pedagogy in Early Years is the result of this research or study into Pedagogical Effectiveness in Early Learning. Part of the research methodology was the use of reflective dialogues. A reflective dialogue is 'a two way discussion between research partners […] intended to uncover significant thinking about day-to-day practice through the process of scaffolded discussion'. The partners use a video as a shared source of information and draw on each other to extend and develop their shared thinking about practice. This is explained in Appendix C of the SPEEL study.

Rodd, J. (1998), *Leadership in Early Childhood*, 2nd edn. Oxford University Press.

  This book takes you through the skills considered necessary for effective leadership. It defines leadership and covers relationships, team-building, communication and interpersonal skills, the importance of research, managing change and partnerships with parents and the community.

References

Aubrey, C., Godfrey, R., Harris, A. and Dahl, S. (2006), *How do They Manage? An Investigation of Early Childhood Leadership*. Early Childhood Research Unit, University of Warwick.

Bennett, N., Wise, C., Woods, P. and Harvey, J. (2003), 'Distributed Leadership: A Review of Literature'. *National College for School Leadership*. Available at: http://www.ncsl.org.uk/publications/publications-distributedleadership.cfm#distributed (accessed March 2006).

Day, C., Harris, A., Hadfield, M., Tolley, H. and Beresford, J. (2000), *Leading Schools in Times of Change*. Oxford University Press.

DfES (2005), *Key Elements of Effective Practice* (KEEP). London: DfES.

Early Education Support (2006), *The Reggio Emilia Approach to Early Years Education*. Learning and Teaching Scotland. Available at: http://www.ltscotland.org.uk/earlyyears/resources/publications/ltscotland/reggioemilia.asp (accessed January 2007).

Rodd, J. (1998), *Leadership in Early Childhood*, 2nd edn. Oxford: Oxford University Press.

Siraj-Blatchford, I. and Manni, L. (2006), *Effective Leadership in the Early Years Sector (ELEYS) Study*. Institute of Education, University of London.

Siraj-Blatchford, I., Sylva, K., Muttock, S., Gilden, R. and Bell, D. (2002), *Researching Effective Pedagogy in the Early Years* (REPEY). DfES.

Sylva, K., Helhuish, E., Sammons, P., Siraj-Blatchford, I. and Taggart, Brenda (2004), *The Effective Provision of Pre-School Education (EPPE) Project: A Longitudinal Study*. DfES.

Developing Your Context: Where Do We Go from Here?

12

Chapter Outline

Introduction	221
The improvement cycle: a framework for improving play in your setting	222
Envisioning the play provision for your setting	224
Completing an audit	224
Writing a policy for play	226
Writing a development plan for play	226
Writing action plans for play	227
Evaluation	228
Personal learning and development	229
Summary, Further reading, References	231

Introduction

> In order for educators to find a way forward, they need to analyse their current provision, what is actually happening and what they might like to improve, what is possible in the short-, medium- and long-term, how changes can be implemented and how goals can be realized. For some educators, this may mean building on existing good practice, whilst for others it may involve a wholesale reconceptualization of what they are doing, how and why (Wood and Attfield 1996: 155).

This book has introduced you to the elements involved in developing play in your setting: how children learn and develop, key ideas and influences, play as an effective medium for learning, the role of the adult. From now on, work in your setting involves revisiting all these elements and evaluating the impact of your practice on the quality of children's play and learning. This is an ongoing process and forms a cycle of improvement. You have been provided with information, frameworks, activities and further study to help you in the process. We now consider the improvement cycle in more depth.

In this chapter you will be introduced to the concepts of envisioning and action planning, which include goals for development, success criteria, resourcing and time frames, at an individual and whole-setting level. You will be asked to reflect on the key elements of good practice introduced earlier in the book and the outcomes of previous professional development activities. You will reconsider the initial evaluation of your setting and the needs analysis, carried out in the Introduction and Chapter 6, and consider your new position.

Purpose of this chapter

To help you:

- understand the cycle of improvement
- evaluate your practice, knowledge and understanding
- identify action for your future personal development

The improvement cycle: a framework for improving play in your setting

All this section is to be completed as a team.

Figure 12.1 is a general framework that outlines the process for improving play in your setting. Each box in the framework is numbered to help you through the process and is based on the principle of a shared vision for play, which is translated into action. It starts by asking the basic question, 'What do we want for our children?' (1) This is translated into three questions about play (1a, 1b, 1c). This is followed by forming a statement of intent (1d), completing an audit (2), developing a policy (3), identifying goals (4), deciding upon action to achieve those goals (5) and concluding with evaluation (6). The process should be kept simple and embedded into leadership and management activity as described in the previous chapter. (See the final section of Table 11.1 in Chapter 11.) It is assumed the whole team is involved but the manager is the lead practitioner operating in accordance with the key principles for leadership and management in Chapter 11.

Figure 12.1 is a step-by-step guide through the improvement process

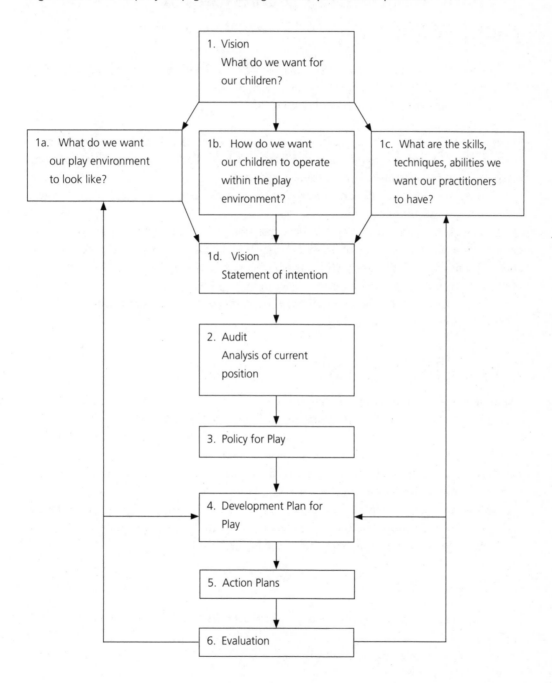

Envisioning the play provision for your setting

> The learning organization is one that engages in the active process of envisioning, a collab-
> orative activity to design and describe the future that reflects the collective aims and aspirations
> of those making up the organisation (Whitaker 1997: 32).

Developing a vision for play requires you to consider your future desirable position by asking
the question 'What do we want for our children?' It will take time and involve reflection,
discussion and re-working before reaching agreement.

Consider questions 1a, 1b, 1c of the improvement cycle diagram in Fig. 12.1, which will
help you to formulate your vision.

Create an ideas map, for each of the above questions, by writing five or six goals that best
describe what you want for the future. Share, discuss and define your meaning for each of the
goals. (You might do this by asking the question 'What will this look like?' or 'How will we do
this?') Fig. 0.1 in the Introduction gives an example of an ideas map.

For each question write a concise statement that summarizes your goals or intentions. This
becomes your vision statement (1d).

Completing an audit

The audit is a review and involves describing and evaluating your current position for each of
the three questions (1a, 1b, 1c). You have already completed your audit for questions 1a and
1b in Chapter 6 when you evaluated your provision, knowledge and understanding against
the key indicators for play from Chapter 4. You also described the practice in your setting and
the role the practitioners take. The next step is to evaluate the role of the practitioner in order
to complete the audit (question 1c).

Now use the same headings to evaluate your practice. Use the key questions provided below
and evaluate by indicating, where appropriate, whether each item is a strength, satisfactory or
a weakness. Identify evidence to support your judgement.

Provision

How well does the organization of the physical environment, both indoors and outdoors:

- ensure a balance and range of play experiences?
- allow children to invent, explore, create and revisit learning?
- allow children to make choices, be independent, work comfortably, move about, concentrate, be

noisy or be quiet?

- What evidence do you have?

Resources (equipment and consumables)

- How much play potential do the equipment and materials have?
- To what extent do resources enable children to demonstrate skills at their 'highest level'?
- How suitable is the range of resources for children to pursue their interests?
- What evidence do you have?

Planning

- How well does planning take account of observations and assessments?
- To what extent does planning ensure continuity and progression in children's learning?
- How proficient is the team in planning for play?
- To what extent does planning involve the views of parents and children?
- What evidence do you have?

Interactions

- How often and how well do practitioners engage in shared sustained thinking with the children?
- How well do practitioners support children's learning?
- What evidence do you have?

Observation, monitoring and assessment

- How skilled is the team in making observations and assessments?
- How well do systems for recording, storing and retrieving information about children's play and learning work?
- How involved are the children in assessing their learning?
- What evidence do you have?

Management

- How effective are your policies and procedures for each of the above areas?
- How effective is practitioner professional development in relation to their understanding and use of play?
- What evidence do you have?

Writing a policy for play

Writing a policy for play involves drawing up a set of principles relevant to your own context. Action to achieve your vision for play is based on these principles.

Approach this by:

- referring to your audit of your current position (see Chapter 6)
- referring to your ideas map (see above)
- revisiting Activity 7.1 to remind you of the policy-making process
- referring to Appendix 1, an example of a policy for play (your policy will, however, reflect your own context and include statements relevant to your setting)
- using key headings and bullet-point format

Your policy should include: a rationale for why you consider it important for children to learn through play; a vision statement, goals, resources and support needed to achieve the goals; how you will communicate your vision and procedures for review. Your policy goals may be used as checklists for monitoring or measures for evaluation.

It would be good practice to share your policy with other stakeholders in the nursery, for example, governors.

Writing a development plan for play

The development plan for play prioritizes what you will develop, while action plans demonstrate how you will develop, in order to achieve your vision.

For each question 1a, 1b, 1c identify three goals that you believe to be priorities.
For each goal there should be a lead practitioner (someone who has overall responsibility but will work within a group), a time frame (how long roughly the project will take) and costs.

Table 12.1 is an example of a pro forma you might use for development planning.

Table 12.1 An example of a pro forma for development planning

Key Question	Goal for Development	Time Frame	Lead Practitioner	Cost across the Time Frame
What do we want our play environment to look like?	. . .			
How do we want our children to operate within it?	. . .			
What are the skills, techniques and abilities we want our practitioners to have?	. . .			

Appendix 2 is an example of a completed development plan.

Writing action plans for play

It is important to remember that action planning should be kept very simple. Each goal needs to be broken into manageable parts or projects and should reflect what you need to do in order to achieve that particular element of the goal. (Table 12.2 is an example of a pro forma you might use for action planning.) Changing one small aspect of your practice moves you towards your goal and enables you to monitor impact and identify success more easily. You may have several simultaneous small projects on the go. For example, Mrs Jones is taking the lead in the vegetable garden project but is also part of the group reviewing role-play resources, led by Mrs Smith. You will also notice, from the example given in Appendix 3, that in carrying out the garden project, other goals on the development plan are incorporated, such as improving relationships with parents and developing planning.

Approach writing your action plans by:

- briefly describing your current position for each goal. Talk about your 'needs' in order to achieve the goal
- breaking down the goal for development into manageable tasks or projects

- choosing one project
- writing a project statement for what you want to achieve. You might want to use a phrase, for example, the practitioners/children will be able to....... This is your measure for evaluating how successful you are
- deciding what action you are going to take in order to meet your project statement
- deciding who is going to do what and by when. Your time frame needs to be realistic and within the overall time frame on the development plan. Consider the support required for practitioners to succeed
- monitoring progress. It might be a good idea to set a review date and identify means of monitoring
- deciding how you will evaluate your project and identifying the evidence you will gather

Table 12.2 An example of a pro forma for action planning

Goal for development. Current position	Breakdown of goal into projects	Project statement, e.g. The children/ staff will be able to....	Action to be taken	By whom	Time	Resources or other support	Cost	Progress – review date monitoring, evaluation, evidence

Appendix 3 is an example of an action plan for play.

Evaluation

Improvement in the quality of play is the central purpose of the evaluation process. By now you may have several projects in place but to ensure improvement it is important to look at the impact of the projects on the quality of children's play, learning and development.

Evaluation is similar to assessment in that it asks the questions 'How well is something happening?' and 'What should be done next?' but it also involves gathering evidence to answer, 'How do we know how well we are doing?'

Evaluation is the final part of the improvement cycle reviewing progress and impact against the goals for development for each of the questions (1a, 1b, 1c) in your development plan. Evaluating the quality of practice takes place on two levels, team and individual.

In order to answer the first question 'How well is something happening?' you will need to look at statements or criteria against which you can make a judgement and identify strengths and weaknesses (things that work well, things that don't). Some possible criteria are:

- the principles (outlined in Chapters 7–10)
- policy goals you have identified

- project statements in the action plans that relate to this cycle
- action from your personal learning journal entries, relating to the activities in Chapters 7–10

Some possible sources of evidence to answer the question 'How do we know how well we are doing?' are:

- feedback
  - o from colleagues
  - o from parents and children
- observations and assessments, including:
  - o observations of children's levels of involvement and dispositions
  - o photographs
  - o children's learning journeys
- documentation
  - o policies and planning
  - o personal learning journal record sheets

Evaluation is the final part of the process of observation, reflection, action and evaluation that you have used for your personal learning journal. The next section uses your evaluations to consider future action for your personal development.

Personal learning and development

Your personal learning continuum is a learning journey that begins with your current position. Initially you work with support from a range of sources until independence is reached and you are able to identify and plan your own action for development.

Table 12.3 Personal learning continuum

Audit (Initial Position) – identify strengths and weaknesses	Supported Action – reading, activities, reflections and reviews	Evaluation against initial audit – review strengths and weaknesses (New Position)	Personal action plan

Dependence ◄—————————————————————————————► Independence

Throughout this book you have made entries in your personal learning journal and gathered a range of evidence of your developing understanding.

In the section on personal development in Chapter 6 you reviewed your current practice, knowledge and understanding and identified action for development.

Use your personal learning journal evaluations, your work from chapter activities and reading, to help you revisit this self-audit and identify your new current position. Identify your strengths and weaknesses and prioritize three or four aspects for improvement; these need not all be weaknesses; it may be you have a strength that you wish to build on. Draw up a personal action plan, using Table 12.4 as an example of a pro forma to help.

Table 12.4 An example of a pro forma for personal action planning

Personal Action Plan				
Name:		Time frame:		
Aspect for improvement	Action	Support	When	Evaluation and evidence
I want to be able to……..	I will achieve it by……..	I will need support from…….. (person or other)	I will achieve it by……..	I am doing well at…….. My evidence is……..
Review date:		Next steps:		

This personal action plan is relevant whether you are a practitioner or manager of a setting. However, if you are a manager you will be asking an additional question: 'How well am I managing?' and some of your action for improvement will relate to the leadership and management aspect of your work. You have already created a personal action plan in Activity 11.4. Return to that action plan and, in addition, use the questions below to extend your thinking.

Some questions you may ask yourself:

- How well do I organize and manage my time?
- What do I find challenging about my role and how well do I deal with challenges?
- How well do I empower practitioners to take responsibilities and a lead role in the process of improving play?
- How well do I support practitioners in their professional development?
- How well do parents, the wider community and I work together?
- How well am I implementing the vision for play?

It may be relevant that key people are asked to contribute to your perception of how well you are managing by being given the same questions and invited to give objective and honest feedback.

Summary

You should now have a deeper understanding of the process involved in improving learning through play. It is not just about a series of projects that may change practice and be fun to implement; it is about ensuring any action has a positive impact upon the quality of play and children's learning. In addition, improvement is also about making a commitment to professional development; challenging your current practice, improving knowledge, understanding and skills, changing the way in which you work and questioning the practice of others.

You should now be ready to implement your action plans for achieving this vision alongside your personal development action plan.

Further reading

The following are examples of sources that may support you in improving further your own skills or those of your setting:

- Visits to other settings with a focus for observation and discussion
- Local Authority training
- The Open University
- Further Education and Higher Education Institutions will be able to provide information regarding Foundation, Education Degrees, Continuing Professional Development courses and Masters Degrees (Foundation Degrees are normally full- or part-time work-based degrees that bring institutions and employers together to create work-based and academic learning related to your particular profession. Some institutions offer Masters Degrees based on action research in your own classroom.)
- http://www.foundationdegree.org.uk

References

Whitaker, P. (1997), *Primary Schools and the Future: Celebration, Challenges and Choices*. Oxford: Oxford University Press.

Wood, E. and Attfield, J. (1996), *Play, Learning and the Early Childhood Curriculum*. London: Paul Chapman.

Appendix 1:
Policy for play: what
do we want for our children?

Rationale for play

Play underpins all development and learning for young children. Most children play spontaneously, although some may need adult support, and it is through play that they develop intellectually, creatively, physically, socially and emotionally (DfES, 2007: 7).

Vision statement

At Dingly Dell Nursery we want our children to be independent, confident and active learners who are able, through their play, to work beyond their normal level of operation. Through shared and collaborative play we want them to be socially competent and develop high-level skills of interaction. We will do this by providing a range of challenging and stimulating play experiences within a safe, secure, supportive and inclusive environment that reflects our children's interests, needs and cultures. The children will be supported by reflective practitioners, who understand how children develop and learn and who continually seek to improve their practice and the quality of the children's learning and play environment.

Objectives

We want our children to be independent, confident learners as individuals and within different social contexts. We will do this by:

- respecting children who wish to engage in solitary play but encouraging collaboration and cooperation
- supporting children in pursuing their interests and ideas
- building upon the positive aspects of children's learning
- positively supporting children with their difficulties
- providing an environment that allows children to make choices and pursue their ideas

We want our children to be active learners, manipulate their environment and connect their experiences (indoors and outdoors). We will do this by:

- providing a range of learning experiences
- planning experiences that allow children to use all their senses and move about
- providing opportunities for children to represent their learning in a variety of ways

We want our children to develop their interests and become immersed in their thoughts and ideas. We will do this by:

- providing children with experiences that are relevant and based upon their interests
- providing experiences and learning opportunities that promote problem solving
- giving children time to pursue and revisit their interests

We want our children to make choices and work at their own pace. We will do this by:

- allowing them to choose materials and where they want to play
- giving them time to explore their interests both within the session and during the course of the week

We want our children to pretend and be imaginative. We will do this by:

- planning a range of role-play opportunities
- providing opportunities for socio-dramatic play
- supporting children in playing cooperatively and collaboratively

We want our practitioners to be effective learners themselves. We will do this by:

- becoming proficient in making observations and assessments
- being reflective and evaluative
- engaging in action research
- asking questions

The practitioners will continually improve the quality of the children's learning and environment both indoors and outdoors. We will do this by:

- making observations of children playing
- monitoring the play environment and children's learning within it
- making assessments of the children's learning that will inform our planning for appropriate play experiences

We will endeavour to form effective relationships with the children, their parents/carers and other relevant adults. We will do this by:

- recognizing that parents also play with their children
- sharing achievements with the children, their parents and carers
- encouraging parents/carers and other appropriate adults to become involved in the children's play
- communicating effectively, which will involve:
  - o using the language of play when discussing with staff and parents/carers children's learning and play experiences
  - o interacting effectively with children in order to extend their learning whilst they are playing
  - o communicating with parents and carers about the play experiences provided in the nursery through a variety of means to ensure there is an understanding of how and why we want the children to learn through play

Practitioners will understand how children learn and develop. We will do this by:

- observing children and reflecting upon their learning
- engaging in continuing professional development in order to develop our understanding, knowledge and skills of how children learn through play
- working together to share knowledge and information about the children's play and learning

We want our play environment to be friendly, welcoming, supportive and inclusive. We will do this by:

- recognizing and learning about children's cultures
- encouraging parents and carers to visit the nursery and play alongside their children
- encouraging and listening to parents and carers talk about the children's interests, likes and dislikes

We want our play environment to be safe, secure and promote independence indoors and outdoors. We will do this by:

- adhering to our health and safety policy
- planning and sharing with the children rules and expectations for operating within the setting
- being well organized, clean and tidy
- providing a stress-free environment
- storing resources in such a way that they are accessible to and can be managed by the children

We want our environment to contain high quality resources and materials. We will do this by:

- evaluating resources to ensure effective use
- ensuring resources are appropriate to the interests and development of the children
- ensuring resources are multi-purpose and robust
- prioritizing expenditure and purchasing the best we can afford

We want our environment to reflect the children's interests, needs and culture. We will do this by:

- considering the layout of the nursery to provide the right kind of play environment to match the needs and development of the children
- observing, interacting with and responding to requests from the children regarding their interests
- providing a range of relevant cultural artefacts

This policy will form the basis for monitoring and evaluating the quality of the play environment, play experiences and the role of the practitioner.

Review and Evaluation of the policy will take place yearly. This policy will be evaluated in light of the impact upon children's learning.

Communication – parents and carers will be informed of this policy through the daily practice in the setting and in the nursery prospectus.

Staff will be informed of this policy during their induction. It will underpin their daily practice.

Resources will be allocated according to agreed priorities in order to implement this policy.

References

DfES (2007), 'Practice Guidance for the Early Years Foundation Stage', in *The Early Years Foundation Stage: Setting the Standards for Learning, Development and Care for Children from Birth to Five*. London: DfES.

Appendix 2: Development plan for play

Key Question	Goal for Development	Time Frame	Lead Practitioner	Cost across the Time Frame
What do we want our play environment to look like?	Improve the quality of materials, resources and storage	3 years	Mr T & Manager	£1,000
	Develop outdoor play	3 years	Mrs J & Manager	£2,000
	Improve provision to reflect the children's families and culture	1 year	Mrs S	£200
How do we want our children to operate within it?	Improve the learning experiences and opportunities provided	1–3 years	Mrs S	NA
	Develop and implement a system for planning	1–2 years	Mrs J	NA
	Explore and develop ways of involving the children in decisions about their learning	1 year	Mrs S	NA
What are the skills, techniques and abilities we want our practitioners to have?	Develop relationships with parents	1 year	Mr T	£50.00
	Improve the quality of practitioner involvement with the children	3 years	Mrs L & Manager	£1,500
	Improve practitioners' professional development	3 years	Manager	£3,000

Appendix 3:
An example of an action plan for developing an aspect of your development plan for play

Goal for development:
to develop the outdoor play environment

Current position	Projects to achieve goal *Highlight project for action*	Project statement *The children/ staff will be able to....*	Action to be taken	By whom	Time	Cost	Resources or other support	Progress – review date monitoring, evaluation, evidence
Outdoor area is both concrete and grass. Resources – plastic climbing frame, shed, box of toys, 2 push chairs, 2 tricycles, scooter, plastic sand tray	To create the following areas for outdoor play: Vegetable garden	Children will be able to - grow vegetables and flowers indoors and outdoors - independent-ly access the outdoors to care for, moni-tor and enjoy the vegetable garden - independently access the shed for equipment - access a range of information for extending their interests and learning - share with their parents the vegetable garden	Organize visit to 'Green's Garden Centre' for purchase of seeds, compost, tools, watering cans etc.	Mrs J to organize, Sally and parents to be involved	Wed 15th May	£50.00 £30.00	Hire of mini bus. Purchase of tools, seeds, labels and storage boxes	Monitor children's access and use of garden and resources Monitor outcomes as identified Review date and plan next steps at team meeting 14th July Evaluate against project statement Evidence – photographs observations parent feedback
	Digging patch Quiet corner Role play Large water play Wet and dry sand play Mark making		Prepare growing area	Mrs J, parents and children	Week 6	NA	Digging implements for children. Notice to parents informing of project and key events	
			Organize shed to store tools and wheel-barrows etc.	Mrs J and Sally	Week 5	NA		
			Theme of 'growing' to be planned for weeks 7–11	All staff Next 3 team meetings to plan 'growing' theme	Week 4	NA		
	As a start to developing this area we wish to create a vegetable garden		Open day and tea party to share growing area with parents	Mrs J to organize	12th July	£10.00	Bread, butter, squash etc.	Invite comments from parents on children's response to project

Appendix 4: Additional frameworks for supporting the development of play

Framework for health and safety

The following are guidelines to support you in writing a health and safety policy. You will, however, need to consult appropriate and relevant health and safety regulations.

- Risk assessment is part of everyday procedures; guidelines and pro forma should be in place
- Ongoing checking and maintenance of equipment/materials should be embedded in everyday practice. Guidelines on how to do this and what to do should equipment not be up to standard should be in place
- There should be appropriate equipment/materials for the developmental stage, age and abilities of the children
- There should be appropriate equipment/materials for the activity
- Both of these should be linked with your provision policy
- Rules for use, retrieval and storage of equipment and hygiene should be devised and displayed for everyone to see. They should also be shared with the children
- Children are trained in hygiene and given practice and reminders in using, retrieving and storing equipment/materials
- Children are appropriately supervised. This will vary depending on the activity and the space available to you, e.g. you will need to have a policy for supervision of the outdoor area
- Procedures are in place to cope with inevitable accidents. Procedures should be clearly displayed; first-aid equipment should be stored safely and be accessible. There needs to be a designated first-aid person, training must be kept up to date and there should be an ongoing dissemination of relevant information

Framework for monitoring and reviewing play

Monitoring and reviewing the play provision, children's learning experiences and the role of the adults requires you to engage in certain activities on an ongoing basis and other activities at specific times in the year, e.g. each policy will have a review date, which may come at the end of the year or be spread out across the year. Some activities you will monitor regularly, e.g. observing practitioners and others at particular times of the year, e.g. purchasing of basic resources.

What kinds of things does the manager monitor?

- *The planning, teaching and learning, monitoring and assessment of play*: This will involve the ongoing monitoring of practice in all of these aspects together with the review of any policies, such as procedures for making assessments of play and whether the policy needs changing in light of the developing practice. A review of planned themes will inform the planning of themes for the following year as will the scrutiny of assessments and learning journeys. The success of any projects from action plans will also need to be monitored and reviewed. On a weekly basis the monitoring of children's specific needs will inform structured and guided play, direct teaching and enhanced provision. The scrutiny of children's portfolios in order to track their progress will need to be embedded into the procedures for assessment and will be part of your monitoring cycle. You may achieve this by creating a yearly time line on which you plot your monitoring activity of what needs to be done when. This could be shared and include team monitoring activity

- *Play provision*: This will involve ongoing monitoring of the principles outlined in the provision chapter or your play policy and you may want to develop some kind of checking format in order to help you. On a yearly basis you will review the basic play provision and on a weekly basis the enhanced provision because both inform future planning and spending priorities

- *The deployment of adults*: This will involve the ongoing monitoring of roles and responsibilities and any established rotas and routines as well as regular review in staff meetings

- *The performance of adults, including training and its impact upon play and learning*: The practitioners should come to expect that their 'performance' with the children will be monitored and reviewed alongside other forms of evidence regarding children's progress. This, however, should be part of the continuing professional development process and alongside other sources of information identify practitioner needs in terms of support and training in understanding how children learn through play

- *The involvement and response of parents*: Decisions need to be made about how you will work with parents to share and celebrate children's achievements, how you will involve parents in understanding how children learn through play and how you will gather information from parents about their child's play and learning. Some of this can be monitored informally on a daily basis but other aspects will need formally reviewing

How does the manager monitor play?

The manager monitors play through asking two key questions:

- What is happening? – This requires observation, analysis and reflection, discussion with practitioners, children and other adults and systematic monitoring to consider all viewpoints and aspects
- How well is it happening? – All the things we wish to happen may be happening but this is of little value if it does not improve the learning of the children. We must therefore look at the extent to which things are happening and the impact on children's learning of the play provision, play experiences and adult intervention. We need to use criteria as some kind of measure. This means making systematic observations yourself of child–adult interactions, ensuring there is collaborative review and moderation of children's portfolios against learning and developmental outcomes, asking parents and talking with children about their learning and play experiences, use of inspection (OfSTED) criteria and review against agreed criteria in action plans and policies

Appendix 5:
What the research says:
key research projects in this area

Oxfordshire Pre-school study

The Oxfordshire Pre-school study was directed by Jerome Bruner and was set up to investigate the quality of provision for under-fives in Britain in the 1980s. Five books were produced as a result of the project; of particular interest is *Childwatching in Playgroup and Nursery School: Oxford Pre-school Research Project* (Sylva 1980). This reported the finding that adults who are actively engrossed in tasks with the children provide a unique opportunity to stimulate language and thought and to help children sustain their interest and play more effectively.

SPEEL study

Moyles, J., Adams, S. and Musgrove, A. (2002), *SPEEL: A Study of Pedagogical Effectiveness in Early Learning*. DfES.

The research was set up with the intention of providing a framework of effective pedagogy to be used alongside the Curriculum Guidance for the Foundation Stage. The research investigated the characteristics of effective pedagogy used in the practice of early years practitioners. The resulting Framework has three areas: Practice (context interactions and planning), Principles (entitlements, teaching and learning, roles) and Professional (knowledge, thinking and qualities). Within each section there are key statements about what constitutes good practice.

EPPE project

Sylva, K., Helhuish, E., Sammons, P., Siraj-Blatchford, I. and Taggart, Brenda (2004), *Effective Provision of Pre-School Education (EPPE) Project*. DfES.

The Effective Provision of Pre-School Education Project (EPPE) is a major and very influential piece of research. It was a longitudinal study, commissioned by the DfEE, whose aim was to explore the practices in effective pre-school settings. In particular the project investigated the effects of pre-school education and care on the development of three- to seven-year-olds.

Content of the study

The study asked five questions:

1. What is the impact of pre-school on children's intellectual and social/behavioural development?
2. Are some pre-schools more effective than others in promoting children's development?
3. What are the characteristics of an effective pre-school setting?
4. What is the impact of the home and childcare history on children's development?
5. Do the effects of pre-school continue through Key Stage 1 (ages six and seven years)?

EPPE Summary: Pre-school to end of Key Stage 1 p.2 [internet] accessed April 2007 available at http://www.surestart.gov.uk/publications/?Document=1159

Of particular interest in relation to this book:

The first three sections contain contextual information and information about the design of the research. Section 4 summarizes the characteristics of the parents, families and children prior to the study and section 5 looks at the settings. Section 6 then considers the impact of different types of pre-school settings on children's cognitive progress and their social/behavioural development. In section 7 case studies are presented as part of the findings. Section 8 looks at the effects of pre-school on children's attainment and progress up to the end of Year One. Section 9 answers the key questions about whether pre-school experience leads to lasting gains in cognitive and social/behavioural development to the end of KS1. Section 10 looks particularly at children 'at risk' of Special Educational Needs and Section 11 summarizes the findings of the project.

Methods employed

The EPPE team carried out 12 case studies in centres identified in the middle and upper range of effectiveness, judged on the progress the children made between three and five years, taking into account factors such as home backgrounds and the results of the pre-test at three years old. The study identifies the quality of adult–child verbal interactions, the balance of who initiated the activities, and discipline/behaviour policies in which staff supported children in rationalizing and talking through their conflicts, as key features of excellent settings. Settings that provided good outcomes for children were characterized by high quality adult–child interaction in particular interactions that involve 'sustained shared thinking' and open-ended questioning to extend children's thinking.

The findings also outline the importance of home learning as well as the quality of pre-school on children's development.

REPEY project

Siraj-Blatchford, I., Sylva, K., Muttock, S., Gilden, R. and Bell, D. (2002), *Researching Effective Pedagogy in the Early Years Research: Report RR356*. DfES.

Researching Effective Pedagogy in the Early Years Project (REPEY) was part of the Effective Provision of Pre-school Education (EPPE). The REPEY project was commissioned by the DfES. The project used intensive case studies 'to identify the most effective pedagogical strategies that are applied in the Foundation Stage to support the development of young children's skills, knowledge and attitudes, and ensure they make a good start at school'. Twelve of the settings used in the study were all good or excellent as identified in the EPPE study. In addition, two effective reception classes and 46 child minders judged by local authority experts to be effective were also used. The study looked particularly at adult–child verbal interactions; differentiation and formative assessment; parental partnership and the home education environment; and discipline and adult support in talking through conflicts.

The research showed that adult–child interactions involving 'sustained shared thinking' seemed to be especially valuable in terms of children's learning, and while most effective settings encourage 'sustained shared thinking', excellent settings used this approach much more. They concluded that, 'Our investigations of adult–child interaction have led us to the view that periods of "sustained shared thinking" are a necessary pre-requisite for the most effective early years settings, especially where this is also encouraged in the home through parent support.' The research also found that 'practitioners extending child-initiated interactions' was also a feature of excellent settings as was adult 'modelling' and open-ended questioning which were all associated with better cognitive achievement.

Read a summary for yourself:

Iram Siraj-Blatchford, Kathy Sylva, Stella Muttock, Rose Gilden, and Danny Bell, *Researching Effective Pedagogy in the Early Years*, DfES [internet] available at http://www.dfes.gov.uk/research/data/uploadfiles/RB356.doc

ELEYS project

Siraj-Blatchford, I. and Manni, L. (2006), *Effective Leadership in the Early Years Sector (ELEYS) Study*. Institute of Education, University of London.

This project is an extension to the work in the REPEY study. It looks at what the literature says about effective educational leadership in the early years and uses the REPEY sample of effective settings to identify the characteristics of effective leadership. It concludes that as well as understanding the context, commitment to collaboration and the improvement of children's learning outcomes there are other 'categories of effective leadership practice' such as a collective vision and goals, effective communication, reflection and ongoing professional development, monitoring and assessing practice, teamwork, and strong community and parent partnerships.

Early childhood leadership project

Aubrey, C., Godfrey, R., Harris, A. and Dahl, S. (2006), *How Do They Manage? An Investigation of Early Childhood Leadership*. Early Childhood Research Unit, University of Warwick.

This study worked with a range of settings to establish the meaning of leadership, the factors contributing to effectiveness, staff training needs and how to build knowledge, skills and capacity in the leadership field. The researchers found that settings tend to be hierarchical in structure but collaborative in culture; a range of leadership roles is adopted; characteristics of leadership vary according to professional qualifications and background. There is a need to develop reflective and strategic skills, to increase self-understanding and problem-solving leadership skills in all early childhood staff and to consider distributed leadership as a way forward in enhancing teamwork and professional development practice. Of particular significance to this book is the finding that, 'A significant positive relationship was found in the survey analysis between delivering quality service and seeing professional development as important' (p.9).

Find the report at: http://www.esrcsocietytoday.ac.uk/ESRCInfoCentre/ViewAwardPage. aspx?AwardId=3802

Appendix 6: Current government documentation

DfES (2007), *Statutory Framework: Setting the Standards for Learning, Development and Care for Children from Birth to Five* and *Practice Guidance for the Early Years Foundation Stage: Setting the Standards for Learning, Development and Care for Children from Birth to Five.* HMSO.

These two documents set out the statutory framework and the practice guidance for the early years foundation stage, which ensures children of 0–5 achieve the five Every Child Matters outcomes of staying safe, being healthy, enjoying and achieving, making a positive contribution, and achieving economic well-being. They set out the requirements for 'Learning and Development and Welfare' for children in maintained and non-maintained schools, independent schools and with registered childcare providers. There are four key principles intended to guide the work of practitioners: A Unique Child, Positive Relationships, Enabling Environments, Learning and Development.

The CD-Rom is also included; this contains all the information in the printed documents plus further examples of practice and links to other useful resources.

Index

abstract thinking   35
action planning   149, 151, 216–8, 228, 230–1, 237
professional development activities   4–6
altruistic behaviour   63, 68
assessment   19, 27, 111, 115–33
   definition   116
   principles   118–21
   procedures   122–31
Athey, Chris   37, 46–7, 52
audits
   of play   222
   of practice   105, 108, 224
   of role of practitioner   224
autonomy   50, 159

behaviour
   altruistic   63, 68
   and culture   57, 62
   gender   74, 97
   inappropriate   163, 173–4, 242
   learning   43, 47–8, 94
   observation of   19, 116
brain
   development   31–2, 50, 57, 61, 73, 164
   emotion and motivation   32
   function   31–2
   health   58
   and language   40
   and play   91, 95, 98
Broadhead, Pat   1, 28, 139
Bronfenbrenner, Urie   55

Bruner, Jerome Seymour   33, 35–6, 42–3, 47, 59, 87, 90, 156, 165, 170, 180

challenge level of   44, 46, 95, 116–7, 128, 156, 160, 170, 174, 181–2, 188, 196
child initiated activities   82, 87, 143, 152, 159, 164, 170, 242, 243
children's narrative   37, 167–8, 170
Claxton, Guy   44
cognitive
   development   30–53, 59, 80, 242–3
   metacognition   35, 167
   processes   61, 91, 98, 103, 167
constructivism   33
continuum
   intervention   157
   leadership   202
   personal learning   4–5, 229
   planning   181–4
   play   87–9
   recording   122
   scaffolding   156
   social context   96
conversation   166–7
   instructional   43
criteria for good quality play   106, 228
culture   33, 38, 40, 55–7, 67, 235
   and gender   62
   and language   38, 40–1, 57, 62, 75, 92
   and thinking   39, 43, 92
curriculum   40, 120, 138, 151, 184–6
   Guidance for the Foundation Stage   121

internal 165
cycle
  of dependency 159
  improvement 221–4
  monitoring 239
  observation assessment and interaction 19,
    180, 201

development 50, 67–8, 73–4
  brain 31–2, 57
  emotional and social 56, 62, 75, 174
  influences on 54–69, 79–80
  intellectual 38–53, 58, 75, 79
  language/experience 50, 57–8, 62, 167
  mathematical 49
  and parental partnership 121
  physical 58–9
  play 60, 63, 138
dialogue
  internal 75
  shared 158
display 146, 215

Early Years Foundation Stage 138, 147, 245
ego centric speech 39, 62, 77
emotional intelligence 62, 67, 99
environment 21, 23, 46, 50, 56, 57, 58, 60–3,
    68, 74, 92, 101, 110, 116–17, 120, 134–53,
    224, 232–5
Effective Provision of Pre-School Education (EPPE)
    Project 30, 80, 170, 184, 219, 241–3
first hand experience 33, 43, 49, 81
frameworks
  health and safety 238
  effective management and leadership 204
  effective observation 21
  planning meetings 195
Froebal, Friedrich 94

gender 56, 59, 60, 62, 64–5, 74, 97

health and safety 20, 135, 141, 144, 238
High/Scope 46, 146
Hutt, Corinne 104

ideas maps 8, 9, 31, 49, 55, 67
instructive learning environments 118, 134–5
intelligence multiple 44
interaction 163–71
  assessment 119, 122
  evaluating 166
  function of 166–7
  and gender 97
  and learning 35–6, 39–42, 57, 166–7
  principles 165
  quality 165, 242
  social 93
  strategies 165
  sustained shared thinking 170–1, 243
intervention 154–76
  experiential 162–3
  interactive 163–4
  resource based 161–2
  modelling 163
  and behaviour 173–4
  and observation and assessment 19–20, 116,
    119, 127
  planning for 147, 171–5, 180, 182, 184, 186
  principles 160
  strategies 157–8
involvement 21, 44–6, 108, 149, 166, 229
  adult 112, 121, 126
  joint involvement 170

key practitioner 28, 121, 122
key principles
  evaluation against 106
  educational conversation 167
  effective management and leadership 204
  interaction 165
  intervention 160

monitoring and assessment   118

planning   181

quality play environment   137

Laevers, Ferre   46, 112

language

conversation   167

culture and family   33, 39, 41, 57, 67

early language   35, 40–1, 57–8, 62

gender   97

and learning   35, 36–49, 62, 75–6, 167

meta language   41

planning for   147, 182, 191, 196

and thinking   33, 38–9, 241

learning

active   46, 50, 60, 72, 81–2, 91, 134

behaviours   50

collaborative   158, 184

co-construction   164, 170

construction of   32, 33, 50, 78, 139, 157, 164

and culture and family   55, 73–4, 92, 165, 211

dispositions   23, 44–6, 52, 63, 68, 73, 74, 91, 103, 116, 138, 143

effective   18, 62, 70, 95, 106, 219

and emotion   32, 62–3

enactive   37

and experience   50–1

gender   97

iconic   37

influences on   54–67, 73

and language   38–40, 50, 62, 75, 167

modes   36–8, 47, 91, 183

and representation   36, 50, 76

symbolic   37

stories   23

learning stories   23

management

key principles of   204–211

of observations   20, 23

of the context   111, 201, 202, 225

of the learning environment   142, 143, 145, 147, 151

personal   126, 203, 217, 218, 230

of the team   209, 211, 212–17

monitoring   206, 239, 240

meta language   41, 49

modes of expression   57, 92, 95

monitoring   115, 116, 117, 179, 182, 201

key principles and framework   118, 239–40

of the context   111, 212–16, 224–5, 228

personal   67

policy   124–6, 233, 235

provision   149, 151

of practitioners   203, 206, 208, 210

motivation   34, 46, 87, 91, 103, 131, 159, 171, 183

Moyles, Janet   41, 53, 86, 104, 219, 241

observation   18–20, 35, 37, 48, 50, 59, 96, 102, 117, 142, 143, 161, 176

and assessment   115–16, 118, 119, 122, 124, 125, 132, 184

and children's thinking   79, 160

and developing the context   111, 225, 229, 231, 233

and intervention   171, 172, 174

and planning   182, 184, 186, 189, 193, 195

Bruner, Jerome   43

ethics   24

use of information   27

management of   205, 212, 214, 240

methods of   21–6, 64–7, 77, 127, 128, 129, 131

of talk/interaction   77, 78, 164, 165, 168

of the learning environment   135, 136, 137, 149, 150

Piaget, Jean   33

parents/carers   20, 117, 121, 122, 124, 130, 184, 204, 205, 234, 235

physical environment   17, 110, 224

importance of   74, 134, 135, 152, 173

Piaget, Jean   33, 35, 36, 47, 49, 60

planning   17, 19, 55, 179–97, 201, 233, 241

action and development   222, 223, 226–30, 236, 237

and assessment   122, 123, 127, 132

and developing the context   111, 225

and intervention   173

for individual needs   74, 79

framework   195

key principles   181–84

management of   208, 211–13, 216–18, 239

the play environment   137–9, 142

process of   185–194

provision   64, 146–8, 151

play

associative   97

collaborative   26, 93, 97, 117, 140, 173, 232

construction   161

continuum   87–9

cooperative   97

creative   101

definitions   86–7

ecology of   134, 152

exploratory   92, 98

free flow   87, 103, 117

guided   87, 89, 239

heuristic   98

imaginative   95, 98, 99, 106

mastery   92

onlooker   96

outdoor   101, 104, 138, 142, 147, 236, 237

parallel   92, 96, 182

participatory   119

physical   99, 101, 104, 185

pretend   92, 98

quality   91, 95, 96, 104, 106, 107, 118, 136,

137, 138, 139, 149, 150, 163–4, 173, 189, 203, 204

role   47, 55, 94, 101, 120, 138, 142, 146, 161, 167, 168, 188, 206–7

sand   138

solitary   96, 182

structured   87, 88

symbolic   92

water   161

with natural materials   100, 104

playful teaching   87, 88, 89, 103, 123, 201

policy   118, 124–6, 132, 182, 203, 212, 226, 232–5, 238, 239

personal development, Practitioners'   3, 111, 112, 218, 229–31

principles   99, 226

evaluation of the setting   106–10

interaction   165–73

intervention   160

learning environment   137–46

management and leadership   204–11

monitoring and assessing   118–21, 126

planning   181–4

problem solving   41, 42, 98, 99, 139, 166, 174, 182

professional development   4, 5, 8, 205, 214, 225, 230, 231, 239

provision   17–21, 27, 47, 50, 64–5, 67, 95, 97, 99, 100, 106, 108, 109, 110, 117, 120, 121, 134, 135, 138–45

areas   146–53

theme free role play areas   139

questioning   39, 44, 45, 119, 156, 168, 177

recording   18, 19, 21–3, 64, 118, 122–3, 126–30, 192

Reggio Emilia   177, 205, 220

Relationships   56–7, 62, 68, 73, 203, 218, 219, 234

Researching Effective Pedagogy in the Early years
(REPEY)   135, 243

Representation   36–7, 40, 43, 52, 75–8, 81, 93,
95, 106, 177

Resources   42, 120, 136, 138–9, 146–53, 225,
226, 228, 235
types of play   87, 88, 99, 100, 101
choosing   81
enactive   37
iconic   37
intervention   158, 161–3, 173, 174
management   110
observation of   18, 20, 21
planning   190–6, 208
storage   140–5
symbolic   37

role of practitioners in play   110–11

scaffolding   42–3, 50, 78, 79, 95, 100, 147, 156,
170, 175, 176, 206

schema   21, 46–8, 52, 79, 81, 92, 95, 106, 142,
180

self management–children's   88

self-regulation–children's   94

self-image   56, 68

self-esteem   56, 62, 63, 66, 68

self-concept   56, 58

self-evaluation   203

self-awareness   3, 5, 62

Siraj-Blatchford, Iram   29, 68, 112, 134, 135,
163, 168, 201, 204, 243

social constructivism   33

social context   26, 60, 67, 96, 104, 121, 167,
184, 193, 195, 232

social interaction   18, 51, 60, 93, 120, 195

spiral curriculum   43, 49, 50, 73, 92, 183, 185

stimulation   32, 56, 57, 74

strategies for
enhancing play provision   149
ensuring appropriate behaviour   173
facilitating learning   167
interaction   165
intervention   157, 163
supporting discussion   109
observation   23

sustained shared thinking   20, 43, 143, 157, 170,
174, 193, 243

talking with children   167, 240

target child   4, 26, 48, 66, 103, 180, 189

teamwork   203, 204, 207–10, 244

theory of mind   35, 36, 97, 98

tools for learning   142

tools of the mind   39

United Nations Declaration of the Rights of the
Child   86

values and aims   110

values   5, 10, 110, 119, 125, 182, 201, 204, 208,
218

vision   9, 107, 202, 204, 206, 211, 216, 218,
222, 223, 224, 226, 230, 232, 243

Vygotsky, Lev Semyonovitch   33, 35, 39, 41, 42,
49, 53, 55, 60, 85, 91, 93, 104, 165

whole child   60, 79, 182, 183

zone of proximal development (ZPD)   41, 42, 46,
50, 91, 95, 99, 156, 160, 171